T0332722

TypeScript for Beginners

TypeScript for Beginners

TypeScript for Beginners

The Ultimate Guide

Sufyan bin Uzayr

CRC Press
Taylor & Francis Group
Boca Raton London New York

CRC Press is an imprint of the
Taylor & Francis Group, an **informa** business

First edition published 2022
by CRC Press
6000 Broken Sound Parkway NW, Suite 300, Boca Raton, FL 33487-2742

and by CRC Press
2 Park Square, Milton Park, Abingdon, Oxon, OX14 4RN

CRC Press is an imprint of Taylor & Francis Group, LLC

Reasonable efforts have been made to publish reliable data and information, but the author and publisher cannot assume responsibility for the validity of all materials or the consequences of their use. The authors and publishers have attempted to trace the copyright holders of all material reproduced in this publication and apologize to copyright holders if permission to publish in this form has not been obtained. If any copyright material has not been acknowledged please write and let us know so we may rectify in any future reprint.

Trademark Notice: Product or corporate names may be trademarks or registered trademarks and are used only for identification and explanation without intent to infringe.

ISBN: 9781032067582 (hbk)
ISBN: 9781032067575 (pbk)
ISBN: 9781003203728 (ebk)

DOI: 10.1201/9781003203728

Typeset in Minion Pro
by KnowledgeWorks Global Ltd.

Contents

CHAPTER 2 ■ Key Concepts of TS 47

Acknowledgments

There are many people who deserve to be on this page, for this book would not have come into existence without their support. That said, some names deserve a special mention, and I am genuinely grateful to:

- My parents, for everything they have done for me

- My siblings, for helping with things back home

- The Parakozm team, especially Aruzhan Nuraly and Madina Karybzhanova, for offering great amounts of help and assistance during the book-writing process

- The CRC team, especially Sean Connelly and Jessica Vega, for ensuring that this book's content, layout, formatting, and everything else remains perfect throughout

- Reviewers of this book, for going through the manuscript and providing their insight and feedback

- Typesetters, cover designers, printers, and everyone else, for their part in the development of this book

- All the folks associated with Zeba Academy, either directly or indirectly, for their help and support

- The programming community in general, and the web development community in particular, for all their hard work and efforts

Sufyan bin Uzayr

About the Author

Sufyan bin Uzayr is a writer, coder, and entrepreneur with more than a decade of experience in the industry. He has authored several books in the past, pertaining to a diverse range of topics, ranging from history to computers/IT.

Sufyan is the Director of Parakozm, a multinational IT company specializing in EdTech solutions. He also runs Zeba Academy, an online learning and teaching vertical with a focus on STEM fields. He specializes in a wide variety of technologies, such as JavaScript, Dart, WordPress, Drupal, Linux, and Python, and he holds multiple degrees, including ones in management, IT, literature, and political science.

Sufyan is a digital nomad, dividing his time between four countries. He has lived and taught in universities and educational institutions around the globe. He takes a keen interest in technology, politics, literature, history, and sports, and in his spare time, he enjoys teaching coding and English to young students.

Learn more at sufyanism.com.

CHAPTER 1

TypeScript

Introduction to TypeScript

TypeScript (TS) is a typed extended set of JavaScript (JS) that compiles to plain JS. As an analogy, if JS was CSS, then TS would be SCSS.

All valid JS code you write is also valid TS code. However, by using TS, you get to use static typing and the latest features that compile into simple JS that is supported by all browsers. TS aims to solve the JS scaling problem, and it works pretty well.

In this book, you'll start by reading about the various features of TS and why learning it is a good idea. The rest of this book will focus on installing and compiling TS, along with some popular text editors that offer you support for TS syntax and other important features.

WHAT IS TS?

TS is a kind of updated version of the JS language. It can run on Node.js or any web browser that supports ECMAScript 3 or higher. TS is a statically compiled language that provides optional static typing, classes, and an interface. It allows you to write simple and clean JS code. So, adopting TS can help you create more easily deployable and more reliable software.

A BRIEF HISTORY OF TS

TS development began in late 2012. Although it originated in Microsoft, and its actual creator is the programmer Anders Hejlsberg, also known as

DOI: 10.1201/9781003203728-1

the creator of such languages as Delphi and C#, this project immediately began to develop as an OpenSource. And from the very beginning, the new language began to spread rapidly due to its flexibility and performance. A lot of projects that were written in JS were transferred to TS. The popularity and relevance of the ideas of the new language has led to the fact that a number of these ideas will later become part of the new JS standard. And the new version of one of the most popular frameworks for web – Angular 2/4/5/6 is completely written in TS jointly by Microsoft and Google.

WHY SHOULD YOU CHOOSE TS?

However, it would seem that there is no need for another programming language for the client side in the web environment, if traditional JS, which is used on almost every site, which is owned by many developers and whose support in the programming community is quite high, also copes with all the same work. But TS is not just a new JS.

First, it should be noted that TS is a strongly typed and compiled language, which may be closer to programmers of Java, C#, and other strongly typed languages, although the output of the compiler creates the same JS, which is then executed by the browser. However, strong typing reduces the number of potential errors that could occur when developing in JS.

Second, TS implements many of the concepts that are common to object-oriented languages, such as inheritance, polymorphism, encapsulation, access modifiers, and so on.

Third, the potential of TS makes it faster and easier to write large complex programs, and therefore easier to maintain, develop, scale, and test them than in standard JS.

Fourth, TS develops as an opensource project and, like many projects, is hosted on GitHub. Repository address – https://github.com/Microsoft/TypeScript. In addition, it is cross-platform, which means that we can use both Windows and macOS or Linux for development.

At the same time, TS is a superset of JS, which means that any JS program is a TS program. In TS, you can use all the constructs that are used in JS – the same operators, conditional, cyclic constructs. Moreover, the TS code is compiled in JS. Ultimately, TS is just a tool that is designed to make application development easier.

Although this language does not provide additional functionality in the runtime, it offers a number of features that help developers write more reliable and easier-to-maintain code than in the case of pure JS.

How Does TS Help Developers Code Easier?

As its name suggests, it adds a type system to JS. If in JS the type of a variable is assigned dynamically, then in TS we have to predefine its type immediately at the time of declaration.

If we are talking about JS, then you can first assign an integer value to a variable, and then reassign it to a string value.

```
let jsVar = 0;
jsVar = "js";
```

In the case of TS, you can restrict this behavior by declaring the type for the variable explicitly. As a result, if you try, for example, to assign a string to a variable of type number, an error will occur.

```
let tsVar: number = 0;
tsVar = "ts"; //error
```

In fact, this is what distinguishes TS from JS. It uses types, which allows us to avoid stupid errors in the code.

How Exactly Does TS Improve JS?

The lack of typing cannot be called a disadvantage of JS, but it gives programmers too much freedom, which inevitably leads to writing code with errors.

```
let aNumber = 123;aNumber = {
name: "Sufyan",
age: 29
}
```

In the JS example above, nothing prevents the developer from presenting the object via the aNumber variable. This approach, although it will not cause the program to crash, will completely eliminate the possibility of self-documenting the code at the expense of variable names.

TS easily solves this problem by defining the type of a variable when it is declared, without further assigning it to a value of another type.

```
let aNumber: number = 123;
```

If this variable is later accessed by another developer, they can be sure that its value is a number, as the name suggests.

```
function isEligible(personObj) {
return personObj.age > 34;
}
let john = {
name: "Josh",
age: 23
};
isEligible(john);
```

In this case, the isEligible function expects an object with the age field. But in JS, there is no way to guarantee that the passed argument will be exactly an object, or that it will contain the age field.

Again, TS has a solution for this.

```
interface Person {
name: string;
age: number;
}
function isEligible(personObj: Person) {
return personObj.age;
}
let john = {
name: "Josh",
age: 23
};
isEligible(john);
```

So far, this code may not be clear to you. But note that it guarantees that the passed variable has the type Person, which is defined at the beginning.

Using TS will save you from hundreds of careless errors in the code, which sometimes turn out to be so stupid that you want to tear your hair out. In addition, your code will become better self-documented and easier to maintain.

If you didn't have enough auto-substitution options for JS code in the integrated development environment (IDE), then you should get acquainted with TS all the more. The presence of types gives this language the ability to offer more precise substitutions in the IDE.

TS AS COMPARED TO JS

What Is JS?

JS was introduced in 1995 as a loosely typed scripting language developed by Netscape to add more dynamics to HTML pages. But the web has changed a lot since then. What were simple pages with a single form in 1995 are now large and complex web applications. JS was not originally designed for developing complex enterprise applications. Currently, most browsers support the ECMAScript 5 standard. That is, usually when someone says "JavaScript," he means the language of the ES5 standard, although ES5 is not the latest version of the standard. In 2015, the 6 standard ES6 was introduced, in 2016 — ES7 or ES 2016. But not all browsers fully support the new features.

The incompatibility problem can be solved by using transpilers such as Babel or using the TS language.

TS Strengths

The main argument in favor of TS is strict static typing. So, what is the difference between static and dynamic typing? When using static typing, less documentation is required, in fact your code has better documentation. For most of the code, it is very useful that the types of arguments and results of the function execution are documented, always knowing exactly what to expect at the input and output.

Moreover, when you look at your old JS code, many nuances are not clear, you need to study the call chain in detail to understand what type of result will be returned in a certain function. Of course, you can use JSDoc, which allows you to write inline documentation, but it needs to be constantly updated. When using TS, you only have one source of truth.

Also, the advantage of static typing is the possibility of autocompletion in code editors. Writing code becomes easier, because you don't have to constantly go through the documentation and look for the name of the method you need.

Also, refactoring becomes less painful, as the compiler will tell you if something is broken, which will avoid runtime errors. But still there are a couple of drawbacks you need more time to learn and write code at the initial stages, an additional layer of complexity appears, freedom of thought is limited, you cannot just add a property or assign a value of another type. Strict typing does not guarantee that there are no errors in the program.

If you are not familiar with TS/ES6/ES7 and you need to write a small web application from a couple of pages, the fastest way to do this is to use regular JS (ES5). But it is also worth noting that ES5 is considered an outdated (deprecated) version of JS, so it is better for your project and career in general to go deeper into learning the new ES6, ES7, and TS standards. At first, you will be intimidated by all these assemblers and transpilers, but your training costs will be justified if you want to stay in the trend of web development. If you work in a team and you need to create a scalable product that will need to be supported for a long time, write it in TS. Since ES6/ES7 now needs to be translated to ES5, you can use TS instead of Babel, so you will maintain type security and your code will work in all browsers.

TS brings many benefits to performance and to the developer experience. TS is not unique to Angular; other powerful integrated environments, such as React and Vue, are starting to use TS to allow development teams to build applications that are robust, resilient, and scalable. JS and TS are constantly evolving but do not compete with each other. TS was created to complement and improve JS, not replace it. In the future, they may become very similar in function, but for now, TS remains a statically typed alternative.

Syntactic Sugar

TS provides a very simple syntax for checking the type of an object at compile time. This syntax is known as syntactic sugar, or, more formally, type annotation. Consider the following version of our JS source code, written in TS:

```
var test: string = "this is a string";
 test = 1;
 test = function(a, b) {return a + b; }
```

Notice that in the first line of this snippet, we entered a colon: and the string keyword between our variable and its assignment. This type annotation syntax means that we set the type of our variable as a string type and that any code that does not adhere to these rules will result in a compilation error. Running the previous code through the TS compiler will cause two errors:

```
hello.ts(3,1): error TS2322: Type 'number' is not
assignable to type 'string'. hello.ts(4,1): error
TS2322: Type '(a: any, b: any) => any' is not
assignable to type 'string'.
```

The first mistake is pretty obvious. We have specified that the test variable is a string, and therefore trying to assign a number to it will cause a compilation error. The second error is similar to the first one and, in fact, says that we can't assign the function to a string.

Thus, the TS compiler introduces strong or static typing in our JS code, giving us all the advantages of a strongly typed language. Therefore, TS is described as an extended JS variant.

TS STRUCTURE

Microsoft designed TS with specific architectural parameters in mind, which allow TS to integrate fully and easily with existing JS code, while providing robust features external to JS.

1. **Providing a Type Check:** JS, being a freely typed language, is extremely lenient about the value assigned to its variables, and it does not create any structural contracts between these variables and the constructs that use them. Passing a number argument to a function that expects a string parameter does not generate errors in JS at design time, but will create chaos at runtime when the function body fails to use this argument correctly.

   To avoid such problems at runtime, TS was designed as a strongly typed language that performs static type checking at compile time in JS. For flexibility, the TS type-checking capability is optional; however, most of the key benefits of TS are related to type-checking – this is the main reason for using TS! For example, type-checking allows you to use the language service layer of the language to create better tools that maximize performance and reduce errors.

2. **More Powerful Object-Oriented Programming:** The syntactic sugar provided by TS will significantly reduce the amount of code while increasing its expressiveness. TS makes writing an object-oriented code class fast. It provides us with classes, interfaces, and modules that allow us to properly structure code into encapsulated reusable structures, making it easier to maintain and scale. Inside classes, you can also specify the visibility level of class properties and methods using the provided TS modifiers-public, private, and protected. There are many other abstractions that will make you, as a developer, more productive.

3. **Basic TS Compiler:** The main task of the TS compiler is to manage the low-level mechanics of checking the type of code and converting it into valid JS code. The compiler uses static code analysis to reduce the chance of runtime errors. Typos in the code or passing the wrong type of argument to a function will cause the compiler to throw errors to warn us that something is wrong before we execute the code. This is extremely valuable, as even with the most complete set of tests, logical errors and extreme cases can cause the application to crash at runtime. TS ensures that the type definitions we create in the code are always used.

4. **TypeScript Standalone Compiler, TSC:** The stand-alone TS compiler, often called tsc, is a high-level compiler that takes a TS file, .ts, and outputs a JS file, .js.

5. **Language Service:** This component layer sits on top of the main TS compiler and provides the features needed to work in IDE and text editors: statement completion, code formatting and highlighting, syntax highlighting, and more. The language service also provides code refactoring: variable renaming, debugging, and incremental compilation.

6. **Tool Integration:** TS offers type annotations that allow IDEs and text editors to perform comprehensive static code analysis. These annotations allow these tools to make smart suggestions, making the code much more predictable. In turn, IDEs and text editors can offer better auto-completion and refactoring of TS code.

Basic TS Types

TS is a statically typed language. The type cannot be changed during program execution. This allows you to reduce a large number of errors and identify many of them even at the compilation stage.

TS has several simple data types: numbers, strings, structures, Boolean. It supports all types that are available in JS, complementing the convenient enum type.

Boolean

The most basic type is the Boolean true/false, which is called Boolean in JS and TS.

```
let isEnabled = true;
let isAlive: boolean = false;

console.log(isEnabled);
console.log(isAlive);
```

Number

Unlike various object-oriented languages such as Java, C#, and C++, which provide different data types, such as int, float, and decimal, for storing a numeric value, TS has only one numeric data type, called number. A variable with the number data type can contain any numeric literal with floating, hexadecimal, and binary or octal values.

```
let decimal: number = 6;
let hex: number = 0xf00d;
let binary: number = 0b1010;
let octal: number = 0o744;
```

String

Another important part of programs in web pages and servers is text data. As in other languages, TS uses the same "string" notation for such data. Like JS, TS uses double (") or single (') quotes to frame text data.

```
let name: string = "bob";
name = 'smith';
```

You can also use strings with templates, which can be multi-line and have built-in expressions. These strings are surrounded by back apostrophes or quotation marks (') and inline expressions are denoted as ${expr}.

```
let name: string = 'Gene';
let age: number = 37;
let sentence: string = 'Hello, my name is ${ name }.

I'll be ${age + 1} years old next month.'
```

The equivalent of this sentence declaration:

```
let sentence: string = "Hello, my name is " + name +
".\n\n" +
    "I'll be " + (age + 1) + " years old next month."
```

Array

TS, like JS, has arrays of values. The array type can be defined in one of two ways. The first is to denote the type of array elements before []:

```
let list: number[] = [1, 2, 3];
```

The second way is to use the generalization Array<elemType>:

```
let list: Array<number> = [1, 2, 3];
</number>
```

Tuple

The Tuple type gives you the ability to declare an array with a known fixed number of elements that do not have to be of the same type. For example, you want to have the Tuple value as a pair of "string" and "number":

```
// Declare a tuple type
let x: [string, number];
// Initialize it
x = ["hello", 10]; // OK
// Initialize it incorrectly
x = [10, "hello"]; // Error
```

When you get an element with a known idex, the type of that element will be returned:

```
console.log(x[0].substr(1)); // OK
console.log(x[1].substr(1)); // Error, 'number' does
not have 'substr'
```

When an element with an idex outside the known range is received, the Union type is returned:

```
x[3] = 'world'; // OK string type can be assigned
(string | number)
```

```
console.log(x[5].toString()); // OK, 'string' and
'number' both have the toString method
x[6] = true; // Error, boolean is not (string |
number)
```

The Union type will be described later in the Advanced types section.

Tuples Deconstruction
Since tuples use array syntax, they can be deconstructed or disassembled in two ways. The first one, using a simple array syntax, looks like this:

```
console.log('tupleType[0]: ${tupleType[0]}');
console.log('tupleType[1]: ${tupleType[1]}')
```

Here we simply write each property of the tupleType variable to the console, referring to the index in the array, i.e., tupleType[0] and typleType[1]. The output of this code will be as follows:

```
tupleType[0]: test tupleType[1]: false
```

So, we created a tuple with a string and a Boolean value and deconstructed it using array syntax. Note that since we use the array syntax, we can request the third property of this tuple:

```
console.log('tupleType[2]: ${tupleType[2]}');
```

Since our tuple does not have a third property, *typleType[2]* will be undefined, as can be seen from the output of this line of code:

```
tupleType[2]: undefined
```

This is clearly far from perfection. The best way to deconstruct a tuple is to use the array syntax to create the corresponding tuple on the left side of the assignment:

```
et [t1, t2] = tupleType;
console.log('t1: ${t1}');
console.log('t2: ${t2}');
```

Here we define an array of two elements named t1 and t2 and assign this array a tuple value. Then we write t1 and t2 to the console. The output of this code looks like this:

```
t1: test
t2: false
```

This method of deconstructing a tuple is preferred for a simple reason. We can't define an array of elements that exceeds the number of properties in the tuple. Therefore, the code below will not work.

```
let [et1, et2, et3] = tupleType;
```

Here we are trying to deconstruct our tuple of two properties into a tuple of three properties. The compiler will throw an error in this case:

```
error TS2493: Tuple type '[string, boolean]' with
length '2' cannot be assigned to tuple with length '3'
```

Optional Tuple Elements

Like function signatures, we can also have optional tuple elements. This is achieved with the help of the symbol? in the tuple definition:

```
let optionalTuple: [string, boolean?];
optionalTuple = ["test2", true];
console.log('optionalTuple: ${optionalTuple}');
optionalTuple = ["test"];
console.log('optionalTuple: ${optionalTuple}');
```

Here we have a specific variable named optionTuple with a required string property and an optional Boolean property. Then we assign it the value ["test2", true] and write it to the console. After that, we assign the value ["test"] to the same tuple and write the value to the console. Since the second optionTuple property is essentially optional, this code will be compiled cleanly and will produce, as expected, the following results:

```
optionalTuple: test2,true
optionalTuple: test
```

Enum

Enum is a special type borrowed from other languages like C#, C ++, and Java that provides a solution to the special numbers problem. Enum binds a human-readable name for a specific number. As in languages like C#, the enum type is a more convenient way to give clear names to a set of numeric values.

```
enum Color {Red, Green, Blue};
let c: Color = Color.Green;
```

By default, enums start with 0. You can change this by directly specifying a value for one of the enum members. For example, we can start the previous example with 1 instead of 0:

```
enum Color {Red = 1, Green, Blue};
let c: Color = Color.Green;
```

Or even set values for all members:

```
enum Color {Red = 1, Green = 2, Blue = 4};
let c: Color = Color.Green;
```

A convenient feature of enumerations is that you can also get the name of an enumeration member by passing its numeric value. For example, if we have a value of 2 and we want to see what it corresponds to in the Color enumeration described above, we can do it like this:

```
enum Color {Red = 1, Green, Blue};
let colorName: string = Color[2];

alert(colorName);
```

Let's consider the following code:

```
enum DoorState {
  Open,
 Closed,
  Ajar
 }
```

Here we have defined an enum named DoorState to represent the state of the door. Valid values for this door state are Open, Closed, or Ajar.

Under the hood (in generated JS), TS will assign a numeric value to each of these human-readable enumeration values. In this example, the value of the DoorState enumeration.Open will be equal to the numeric value 0. The same is true for the DoorState enumeration.Closed will be equal to the numeric value 1, and the value of the enum is DoorState.Ajar will be equal to 2. Let's take a quick look at how we'll use these enum values:

```
var openDoor = DoorState.Open;
console.log('openDoor is: ${openDoor}');
```

Here, the first line of this code snippet creates a variable named openDoor and sets its value to DoorState.Open. The second line simply writes the value of the openDoor variable to the console. The output will look like this:

```
openDoor is: 0
```

This clearly shows that the TS compiler has replaced the value of the DoorState enumeration.Open to the numeric value 0.

Now let's use this enumeration in a little different way:

```
var closedDoor = DoorState["Closed"];
console.log('closedDoor is: ${closedDoor}');
```

This code snippet uses the string value "Closed" to search for the enum type and assigns the resulting enum value to the closedDoor variable. The output of this code will be as follows:

```
closedDoor is: 1
```

This example clearly shows that the enum value for DoorState is.Closed is combined with the enum value for DoorState ["Closed"], since in both cases the numeric value 1 is returned. Enumerations are a convenient way to define an easy-to-remember, easy-to-read name for a special number. Using human-readable enumerations instead of just throwing around various special numbers in our code makes the purpose of the code more clear. Use a value for the entire application named DoorState.Open or DoorState.Closed is much easier than remembering to set the value to 0 for Open, 1 for Closed, and 3 for Ajar. In addition to making our code more readable and more understandable, using numbers also protects our code base every time these special numeric values change, since they are all defined in one place. The last thing I would like to mention about enumerations is that we can set the numeric value manually, if necessary, as follows:

```
enum DoorState {
    Open = 3,
    Closed = 7,
    Ajar = 10
}
```

Here we have redefined the default enum values to set the value *DoorState. Open* equal to 3, *DoorState.Closed* equal to 7 and *DoorState.Ajar* equal to 10.

String Enums

Another variant of the enum type is a string enumeration, in which numeric values are replaced with strings:

```
enum DoorStateString {
    Open = "open",
    Closed = "closed",
    Ajar = "ajar"
}
var openDoorString = DoorStateString.Open;
 console.log('openDoorString = ${openDoorString}');
```

Here we have an enum named DoorStateString, where each of the enum values is now of type string. The output of this code snippet will be as follows:

```
openDoorString = open
```

As expected, the TS compiler returns the string "open".

Any

We may need to describe the type of variables that we don't know when we write our application. These values can be obtained from dynamic content, such as from a user or from a third-party library. In these cases, we want to disable type checking and allow the values to pass validation at compile time. To do this, you need to use the any type:

```
let's not be sure: any = 4;
notSure = " maybe a string instead";
notSure = false; / / ok, this is definitely boolean
```

The any type is a powerful way to work with existing JS, which allows you to gradually include more and more type checks at compile time. You can expect Object to play the same role as it does in other languages. But variables of the Object type only allow you to assign them any value. You can't call undeclared methods from them, even those that may exist at the execution stage of the program:

```
let looselyTyped: any = 4;
// OK, ifItExists might exist at runtime
looselyTyped.ifItExists();
// OK, toFixed exists (but the compiler doesn't check)
looselyTyped.toFixed();

let strictlyTyped: unknown = 4;
strictlyTyped.toFixed();
```

The any type can also be useful if you know some part of the variable type, but not all of it. For example, you can have an array with elements of different types:

```
let list: any[] = [1, true, "free"];

list[1] = 100;
```

Void
Void is the opposite of Any: the absence of any types. It is most often used as the return type of functions that do not return any value.

```
function warnUser(): void {
   alert("This is my warning message");
}
```

Declaring variables with the void type is useless, because you can only assign them undefined or null values:

```
let unusable: void = undefined;
```

Null and Undefined

The Null and Undefined types correspond to the same types in JS. These types are subtypes for all other types by default.

```
let n: number = null; / / Primitive types can be null
let m: number = undefined; / / Primitive types can be
undefined
let x = null; / / same as x: any = null
let y = undefined; / / same as y: any = undefined
let e: Null; / / Error
let r: Undefined; / / Error
```

If you declare a variable of type null or undefined, then such a variable can only be assigned the value null or undefined, respectively, which has no practical application.

```
let n: null = null; / / Only this value can be
assigned to
n = 1; / / Error!
let m: undefined = undefined;
m = "some string"; / / Error!
```

It is worth noting that if you use the –strictNullChecks compiler directive, null and undefined can only be assigned to a variable of type void and to variables of type null or undefined, respectively. This helps to avoid a lot of mistakes. In this case, if the variable needs to be assigned a value with the string or null or undefined type, you can use the string | null | undefined union type.

Never

The never type represents a type whose value never occurs. For example, never is a type that returns a function that always throws exceptions or that never exits (for example, an infinite loop). Variables can also have this type, for example, in order to never take the value true.

The never type is a subtype of any type. A variable of type never can be assigned to a variable of any other type. On the other hand, there is no such type that will be a subtype of this type, just as a variable of this type cannot be assigned anything other than a variable of the same type (never).

```
function error(message: string): never {
throw new Error (message);
}
/ / The output type of fail() is never
function fail() {
return error ("Something failed");
}
/ / no exit from this function
function infiniteLoop () function: never {
while (true) {
}
}
```

Symbol

The Symbol type is primitive and corresponds to the same type in JS. This type provides unique identifiers that can be used as keys for object properties.

Values of the Symbol type implement a global 'Symbol' object, which has a set of methods and properties that can be called as functions.

```
var secretKey = Symbol();
var obj = {};
obj[secretKey] = "secret message"; / / Symbol as
property
obj[Symbol.toStringTag] = "test";
```

Type Assertions

Sometimes you find yourself in a situation where you know more about the value of a variable than TS does. This usually happens when you know that the type of an entity may be more specific than its current type.

Type assertion is like typecasting in other languages, but it doesn't do any special checks or data restructurings. The type conversion has no effect at the execution stage of the program and is used only by the compiler. TS assumes that the programmer will do all the necessary checks that are required.

The type conversion can be done in two ways. The first is the use of angle brackets syntax:

```
let someValue: any = "this is a string";
let strLength: number = (<string>someValue).length;
```

The second is as-syntax:

```
let someValue: any = "this is a string";
let strLength: number = (someValue as string).length;
```

The two examples given are completely similar. To use one or the other is by-and-large a choice of preference; however, when TS is used in conjunction with JSX, only typecasting via syntax is allowed.

The Let Keyword

The let keyword is new in JS. A variable declared with let will only be visible in the current (local) scope. This avoids a lot of problems in JS. Therefore, it is recommended to use let instead of var wherever possible.

TS Compiler

The TypeScript compiler (also known as "tsc") is the basis of many packages, plugins, and tools that work with TS, although we don't often call the tsc directly, since we configure the behavior of the tsc inside the packers we use.

When we install TS globally npm i-g TS, we get a tool called tsc. If we run this command with the help tsc –help flag, we will see a large number of options that go with it. The main ones that you should pay attention to are the first examples at the top of examples:

```
tsc hello.ts
    tsc --outFile file.js file.ts
    tsc @args.txt
    tsc --build tsconfig.json
```

If we create a *hello.ts* file, write *const four:number = 2 + 2* inside, and then run *tsc hello.ts*, we get a compiled file *hello.js* with the value *var four = 2 + 2;*.

We will rarely use *tsc* in this way, because *tsc* is included in plugins such as Webpack, Parcel, and Angular CLI.

Instead, we use *tsc –init*. It creates a file in the root directory named *tsconfig. json*. It contains all the default values. This is very convenient, because instead of defining all these parameters on the command line when it is called, we define them in this TS configuration file. When we run the tsc command, the compiler will take the settings from *tsconfig. json*.

Also, we can change the configuration settings, for example, change the value of *ourDir* to *./dist*. Now all compiled files should be saved to an external directory *./dist*.

Everything defined in this file will specify which parameters the TS compiler will use when compiling. When TS starts "complaining" about not using enough types, you can start disabling some of these warnings or errors.

Variable Declarations

Let and const are relatively new types of variable declarations in JS. As we mentioned earlier, let is similar to var in some ways, but allows users to avoid some of the common errors encountered in JS. const is an extension of let that prevents variables from being overridden.

Since TS is an add-on to JS, the language also supports let and const. Next, we'll go into more detail about these new variable declarations and explain why they are preferred over var.

var Declarations

The variable declaration in JS always occurs using the var keyword.

```
var a = 10;
```

As you probably understood, we just declared a variable with the name a and the value 10.

We can also declare a variable inside a function:

```
function f() {
    var message = "Hello, world!";
    return message;
}
```

and we also have access to these variables inside other functions:

```
function f() {
    var a = 10;
    return function g() {
        var b = a + 1;
        return b;
    }
}

var g = f();
g(); // returns 11;
```

In the example above, g captures (encloses) the variable a declared in f. At any point where g is called, the value of a will be associated with the value of a in the function f. Even if g is called once and f has finished executing, it is possible to access and modify a.

```
function f() {
var a = 1;

a = 2;
var b = g();
a = 3;

return b;

function g() {
return a;
}
}

f(); // returns 2
```

Scoping

The var declaration has some strange scope rules for those using other programming languages. See the following example:

```
function f(shouldInitialize: boolean) {
    if (shouldInitialize) {
        var x = 10;
    }

    return x;
}

f(true);  // returns '10'
f(false); // returns 'undefined'
```

Some may need to re-look at that example. The variable x was declared inside the if block, and we can access it outside of that block. This is because var declarations are available anywhere inside the function, module, namespace, or global scope that contains them, regardless of the block in which they are contained. Some call it var-visibility or function-visibility. The parameters are also visible inside the function.

These scope rules can cause several types of errors. One annoying problem is that it is not an error to declare a variable multiple times:

```
function sumMatrix(matrix: number[][]) {
    var sum = 0;
    for (var i = 0; i < matrix.length; i++) {
        var currentRow = matrix[i];
        for (var i = 0; i < currentRow.length; i++) {
            sum += currentRow[i];
        }
    }
    return sum;
```

It's probably easy to see that the internal for loop will accidentally overwrite the variable i, because i has scopes inside the sumMatrix function. Experienced developers know that similar errors slip through code review and can be the cause of endless frustration.

Block Viewport

When a variable is declared using let, it is used in block scope mode. Unlike variables declared with var, whose scopes extend to the entire function they are in, block-scoped variables are not visible outside their nearest block or for loop.

```
function f(input: boolean) {
let a = 100;

if (input) {
// Here we see the variable 'a'
let b = a + 1;
return b;
}

// / Error: 'b' does not exist in this block
return b;
}
```

Here we have two local variables a and b. The scope of a is bounded by the body of the function f, while the scope of b is bounded by the if condition block.

Variables declared in the catch block have the same visibility rules.

```
try {
    throw "oh no!";
}
```

```
catch (e) {
    console.log("Oh well.");
}
// Error: 'e' doesn't exist here
console.log(e);
```

Another property of block scope variables is that they cannot be accessed before they are declared. While block scope variables are represented everywhere in their block, there is a dead zone at each point before they are declared. It's just a way of saying that you can't access them before the let statement, and luckily TS will remind you of that.

```
a++; / / it is incorrect to use 'a' before declaring
it;
let a;
```

However, you can still close a variable with a block scope before declaring it. However, an attempt to call such a function before declaring it will result in an error. If you compile to the ES2015 standard, this will cause an error; however, right now TS allows this and will not indicate an error.

```
function foo() {
    //okay to capture 'a'
    return a;
}
// illegal call 'foo' before 'a' is declared
// runtimes should throw an error here
foo();

let a;
```

Re-declaring and Escaping
In the case of var declarations, it doesn't matter how many times you declare the same variable. You'll always get one.

```
function f(x) {
    var x;
    var x;

    if (true) {
      var x;
    }
}
```

In the example above, all the declarations of x actually point to the same x, and this is perfectly acceptable. This is often a source of bugs. So, it's a good thing that the let declarations don't allow this.

```
let x = 10;
let x = 20; / / Error: cannot redefine 'x' in the same
scope
```

Variables don't have to both be block-scoped in TS for the compiler to indicate an error.

```
function f(x) {
let x = 100; / / error: intersects with function
parameter
}

function g() {
let x = 100;
var x = 100; / / error: cannot declare 'x' twice
}
```

This does not mean that a variable with block scope cannot be declared with a variable with scope in the same function. A variable with a block scope just needs to be declared in its block.

```
function f(condition, x) {
    if (condition) {
        let x = 100;
        return x;
    }

    return x;
}

f(false, 0); // returns 0
f(true, 0);  // returns 100
```

The method of introducing a new name in a nested area is called hiding. This is a kind of two-bladed sword, because it can introduce some bugs, as well as get rid of others. For example, imagine how we could rewrite the sumMatrix function using the let variables.

```
function sumMatrix(matrix: number[][]) {
    let sum = 0;
    for (let i = 0; i < matrix.length; i++) {
        var currentRow = matrix[i];
        for (let i = 0; i < currentRow.length; i++) {
            sum += currentRow[i];
        }
    }

    return sum;
}
```

This version of the loop does the summation correctly, because the i of the inner loop overlaps the i of the outer one.

Such concealment should usually be avoided, so that the code is cleaner. But in some scenarios, this method may be ideal for solving the problem. You should use the best solution at your discretion.

Closure of Variables with Block Scope Viewability

When we first touched on the closure of variables with the var declaration, we briefly looked at how variables behave when closed. To better understand the point, imagine that each time a new scope appears, it creates its own "environment" for variables. This environment and its externally captured variables can exist even after all expressions inside the scope have completed their execution.

```
function myFavoriteCity() {
    let getCity;

    if (true) {
        let city = "Seattle";
        getCity = function() {
            return city;
        }
    }

    return getCity();
}
```

Because we have captured the city variable from its environment, we can still access it, despite the fact that the if block has finished executing. Remember our previous example with setTimeout. We ended up needing to use IIFE to capture the state of a variable for each iteration of the for loop. As a result, we created a new variable environment each time for our captured ones. This was a bit of a pain, but thankfully we won't need to do it again in TS.

Let declarations behave very differently when they are part of a loop. Instead of introducing a new environment for the loop, they introduce a new scope for each iteration. Since this is what we did with our IIFE, we can change our old setTimeout example using let declarations.

```
for (let i = 0; i < 10 ; i++) {
    setTimeout(function() {console.log(i); }, 100 * i);
}
```

and as expected, this will print out the following:

0

1

2

3

4

5

6

7

8

9

Constant Declarations

Constant declarations are another way to declare variables.

```
const numLivesForCat = 9;
```

They are the same as let, only, according to their name, their value cannot be changed after they have already been assigned a value once. In other words, all the let scope rules apply to them, but you can't reassign them. The value they are associated with is immutable.

Let or Const?

We have two ways of declaring with similar rules for their scope, so it begs the question of which one to use. The answer will be the same as for most broad questions: it depends on the circumstances.

Applying the principle of the lowest level of privileges, all variable declarations that you do not plan to change in the future should use const. This is because if a variable should not change its value, other developers who are working on the same code should not be able to write the object. This should only be allowed if there is a real need to reassign the variable. Using const makes the code more predictable and understandable when explaining the data flow.

Destructuring

Another innovation from the ECMAScript 2015 standard, which is in TS, is destructuring.

The simplest form of destructuring is using an array:

```
let input = [1, 2];
let [first, second] = input;
console.log(first); // outputs 1
console.log(second); // outputs 2
```

This creates two new variables named first and second. In essence, this is the equivalent of an index call, just more convenient:

```
first = input[0];
second = input[1];
```

Destructuring also works with previously declared variables:

```
// swap variables
[first, second] = [second, first];
```

And with the function parameters:

```
function f([first, second]: [number, number]) {
  console.log(first);
  console.log(second);
}
f(input);
```

You can create a variable for the remaining list items using the ...name syntax:

```
let [first, ...rest] = [1, 2, 3, 4];
console.log(first); // outputs 1
console.log(rest); // outputs [2, 3, 4]
```

Destructuring an Object

You can also destruct objects as shown in the following example:

```
let o = {
    a: "foo",
    b: 12,
    c: "bar"
}
let {a, b} = o;
```

This code creates new variables a and b from o.a and o.b. Note that you can skip c if you don't need it.

Renaming Properties

You can also give different names to the properties:

```
let {a: newName1, b: newName2} = o;
```

If this syntax is a little confusing to you, you can write it in a different way to make it clearer:

```
let newName1 = o.a;
let newName2 = o.b;
```

The confusing thing is that the colon here does not denote the type. The type, if you specify it, still needs to be written after destructuring:

```
let {a, b}: {a: string, b: number} = o;
```

Default Values

Default values allow you to define a property, even if it was not set:

```
function keepWholeObject(wholeObject: {a: string, b?:
number}) {
    let {a, b = 1001} = wholeObject;
}
```

The keepWholeObject function has a variable for wholeObject, as do the properties a and b, even if b is not defined.

Declaring Functions

Destructuring also works with function declarations; you can see an example below:

```
type C = {a: string, b?: number}
function f({a, b}: C): void {
  // ...
}
```

Specifying default values is more commonly used for parameters, and using destructuring for this can look confusing. First of all, you should remember to specify the type before the default value.

```
function f({a, b} = {a: "", b: 0}): void {
// ...
}
f (); // ok, by default {a: "", b: 0}
```

Then, you should remember to give the default value for the optional properties of the destructured parameter when defining the function. Remember also that c was defined with the optional property b:

```
function f({a, b = 0} = {a: ""}): void {
// ...
}
f({a: "yes"}) // ok, by default b = 0
f() // ok, by default is {a: ""}, which also implies b
= 0
f({}) // error, property 'a' should be set in this
case
```

Use destructuring with caution. As the previous example showed, all complex destructuring expressions have many nuances. This is especially true for multi-level nested destructuring, which is really hard to understand even without renaming, default values, and type annotations. Try to keep the destructuring expressions small and simple.

Interfaces

You can see that TS has obtained a lot from C#. Interfaces will be another example of such close collaboration.

An interface is a declaration that is similar to a class but does not have a method implementation. You can use it to describe the properties and methods of objects. At the same time, the interface does not have the implementation of functions and does not have the code itself – it is only necessary for the compiler to evaluate your implementations of the object (let me remind you that the class is also an object). Roughly speaking, an interface is a descriptive structure. Unlike classes, interfaces are uncompilable and live only in TS runtime.

The interface declaration starts with the interface keyword. Then, the name of the interface comes, which is usually started with a capital letter I. This is not a prerequisite for using interfaces, but I recommend that you stick to this convention, if only because it is very convenient.

You can write interfaces anywhere: next to the code, at the beginning of a file, or even in a separate file. I recommend keeping the interface declaration where it is needed. For example, if the interface is used only within a single module (file), then you can safely keep it there. If the interface is used in many modules of the project, it is more appropriate to create a directory type and decompose the interfaces according to the logic there.

Let's consider the simplest example of an interface for an object describing a VPS server:

```
interface IServer {
    hostname: string;
    location: string;
    active: boolean;
    public_address: string;
}
```

Now that we have defined the interface, we can use it in a variable. It is usually customary to say "implement the interface" rather than "use the interface," since the compiler verifies that the interface is implemented correctly. And, in case of an incorrect implementation (there is not at least one property), it will output errors every time you do something wrong. For example, let's forget to specify the public_address property.

```
const server: IServer = {
      hostname: 'Pikachu',
      location: 'RM1',
      active: true
}
// Error → Type '{ hostname: string; location: string;
active: true; }' is not assignable to type 'IServer'.
//          Property 'public_address' is missing in
type '{ hostname: string; location: string; active:
true; }'.
```

The compiler evaluated our initiatives, but did not see the public_address property in our object, that is why it shows an error.

But some structure cannot always be distinguished using only one interface. Of course, in TS, you can use one interface as a type for a property of another interface.

```
interface IPublicAddress {
      netmask: string;
      gateway: string;
      address: string;
}
interface IServer {
      hostname: string;
      location: string;
      active: boolean;
      public_address: IPublicAddress;
}
```

Note that in addition to primitive types and other interfaces, you can describe functions in interfaces. This is done using arrow functions, for example, like this:

```
interface IServer {
      getPublicAddres: () => IPublicAddress;
}
```

At the same time, no one forbids you to specify the parameters of the function:

```
interface ICalculator {
    sum: (a: number, b: number) => number;
}
```

Extending Interfaces

In TS, you can only extend interfaces, not inherit them. The extension is used if you need a new interface to have not only all the properties of an interface, but also have additional or unique properties for that interface.

```
interface IResponse {
    status: number;
}
```

```
interface ISlackResponse extends IResponse {
    ok: boolean;
}
```

Indexed Types

Sometimes you may need to allow storing in an object not only a pre-known number of properties but also a variable, for example, when you implement the interface of a cache. In this case, you don't know the name of the property, but you do know its type.

```
interface ICache {
    size: number;
    first: ICacheItem;
    last: ICacheitem;
    items: {
        [item: string]: ICacheItem;
    };
}
```

Now you can write any value to the items object that has a string type key and an ICacheItem type value.

Interface Implementation

In the case of an object, you simply assign a colon-separated variable to the interface you need as a type and implement it. With classes, it is somewhat different – classes must implement interfaces. If you forget to write an implementation of at least one method, the compiler will throw an error. For example, we will write a cache interface that will be implemented by the class.

```typescript
interface ICacheItem {
    mtime: number;
    content: string;
}

interface IFileCache {
    set: (key: string, value: ICacheItem) => void;
    get: (key: string) => ICacheItem;
}

class FileCache implements IFileCache {
    store = new Map();

    set(key: string, value: ICacheItem): void {
        this.store.set(key, value);
    }

    get(key: string): ICacheItem {
        return this.store.get(key);
    }
}
```

The above is the simplest example of implementing a class, from which it is not entirely clear why an interface is needed here at all, when we could just create a class. Let's get this straight. After writing the interface, we can implement it as many times as we like, for example, for the image storage cache or anything else.

Discriminated Union Types

We put this type in the section of interfaces, because it only applies to interfaces. Discriminated union type returns a new type that contains only the properties that are present in all interfaces.

Below are three interfaces that have one common property, the type of which is represented as a string literal. This is the property that will be represented in the new type.

```typescript
interface Square {
    kind: 'square';
    size: number;
}
```

```
interface Rectangle {
        kind: 'rectangle';
        width: number;
        height: number;
}
interface Circle {
        kind: 'circle';
        radius: number;
}
```

Now let's look at how we can use the discriminated union in practice. As you probably already guessed, we will calculate the area of the shapes that are described using the interfaces.

```
function area(s: Square | Rectangle | Circle): number
{
        switch (s.kind) {
                case 'square': return s.size * s.size;
                case 'rectangle': return s.height *
s.width;
                case 'circle': return Math.PI * s.radius
** 2;
        }
}
```

We could also use if to make the compiler understand which interface we are currently working with.

```
function area(s: Shape): number {
        if (s.kind === 'square') {
                return s.size * s.size;
        }
        // ...
}
```

Now let's talk about the case when the function can take not only a square, rectangle, and circle, but also a triangle. At the same time, there is no corresponding implementation for the triangle. In this case, the compiler will not throw an error if null and undefined are subtypes. However, if they are full-fledged types, we will either have to specify number | undefined as the type returned by the function, or add default in the case of using case, or else in the case of using if.

Working with Interfaces

The easiest way to see how interfaces work is to start with a simple example:

```
function printLabel(labelledObj: { label: string }) {
    console.log(labelledObj.label);
}

let myObj = {size: 10, label: "Size 10 Object"};
printLabel(myObj);
```

The compiler checks the printLabel call. This function takes a single parameter, which requires that the passed object has a property named label, which would have a string type. Note that our object has other properties, but the compiler only checks that it has at least the necessary properties, and their types match the required ones. In some cases, which we will discuss later, TS does not behave so leniently.

We can rewrite this example, this time using the interface to reflect the need for a string-type label property:

```
interface LabelledValue {
    label: string;
}

function printLabel(labelledObj: LabelledValue) {
    console.log(labelledObj.label);
}

let myObj = {size: 10, label: "Size 10 Object"};
printLabel(myObj);
```

The LabelledValue interface is the name that can now be used to set the requirement from the previous example. It still reflects the need for the object to have a string-type property named label. Note that it is not necessary to explicitly state that the object that we pass to printLabel implements this interface, as it would have to be done in other languages. In TS, only the shape of the object matters. If the object that is passed to the function meets the listed requirements, then it is considered suitable.

It is worth noting that type checking does not require that the properties go in a certain order: it is only important that the necessary properties are present and have the appropriate type.

Optional Properties

Not all interface properties may be required. Some exist only under certain conditions, or none at all. Such optional properties are often found, for example, when passing arguments to a function in the form of an object that specifies only a few properties.

```
interface SquareConfig {
    color?: string;
    width?: number;
}

function createSquare(config: SquareConfig): {color:
string; area: number} {
    let newSquare = {color: "white", area: 100};
    if (config.color) {
        newSquare.color = config.color;
    }
    if (config.width) {
        newSquare.area = config.width * config.width;
    }
    return newSquare;
}

let mySquare = createSquare({color: "black"});
```

Interfaces with optional properties are written like normal ones, but each optional property is marked with the symbol ? at the end of the name.

The advantage of optional properties is that you can describe the properties that may be present, and at the same time prohibit the use of those properties that are not part of the interface. For example, if we made a mistake when entering the color name in createSquare, we would get an error message informing us about it:

```
interface SquareConfig {
    color?: string;
    width?: number;
}
function createSquare(config: SquareConfig): { color:
string; area: number } {
    let newSquare = {color: "white", area: 100};
```

```
    if (config.color) {
        // Ошибка: Property 'collor' does not exist on
type 'SquareConfig'
        newSquare.color = config.collor;
    }
    if (config.width) {
        newSquare.area = config.width * config.width;
    }
    return newSquare;
}
let mySquare = createSquare({color: "black"});
```

Read-Only Properties

Some properties should only be modifiable when the object is created. You can specify this by adding readonly before its name:

```
interface Point {
    readonly x: number;
    readonly y: number;
}
```

You can create a Point object by assigning an object literal, but after the assignment, you can no longer change x and y.

```
let p1: Point = { x: 10, y: 20 };
p1.x = 5; // error!
```

TS has a ReadonlyArray<T> type, which is essentially an Array<T> type, from which all methods that modify it are removed, so you can be sure that such arrays will not change after creation:

```
let a: number[] = [1, 2, 3, 4];
let ro: ReadonlyArray<number> = a;
ro[0] = 12; // error!
ro.push(5); // error!
ro.length = 100; // error!
a = ro; // error!
</number>
```

In the last line of the example, you can see that even assigning ReadonlyArray to a regular array is not allowed. However, this restriction can still be circumvented by using typecasting:

```
a = ro as number[];
```

The easiest way to remember when to use readonly and when to use const is to ask whether this feature is needed for a variable or for an object property. With variables, const is used, and with properties, readonly is used.

Checks for Extra Properties

In our first example of using interfaces, TS allowed us to pass {size: number; label: string;} where only {label: string;} was expected. We also learned about optional properties, and how they can be useful when passing arguments to functions.

However, a mindless combination of these two features would allow you to shoot yourself in the foot just like in JS. For example, if you take the last example with createSquare:

```
interface SquareConfig {
    color?: string;
    width?: number;
}

function createSquare(config: SquareConfig): { color:
string; area: number } {
    // ...
}

let mySquare = createSquare({ colour: "red", width:
100 });
```

Note that the argument passed to createSquare is written as colour instead of color. In pure JS, such things do not give errors, but they also do not work as the developer would like.

We can say that this program is correct from the point of view of types, since the types of the width properties are compatible, there is no color, and the presence of an additional color property does not matter.

However, TS makes the assumption that there is an error in this piece of code. Object literals are processed by it in a special way and are checked for the presence of unnecessary properties. This check is done when literals are either assigned to other variables or passed as arguments. If there are any properties in the literal that are not present in the target type, this will be considered an error.

```
// error: 'colour' not expected in type 'SquareConfig'
let mySquare = createSquare({ colour: "red", width:
100 });
```

It is very easy to bypass such a check. The easiest way is to use typecasting:

```
let mySquare = createSquare({ width: 100, opacity: 0.5
} as SquareConfig);
```

If you are sure that the object can have additional properties that will be used in some special way, then there is an even better way – to add a string index. If SquareConfig objects can have color and width properties, as well as any number of other properties, then the interface can be described as follows:

```
interface SquareConfig {
    color?: string;
    width?: number;
     [propName: string]: any;
}
```

We'll discuss indexes later, but for now just note that in this example, SquareConfig can have any number of properties, and if it's not color or width, then their type doesn't matter.

The last way to bypass the check for redundant properties – which may seem a little unexpected – is to assign an object to another variable. Since squareOptions will not pass the check for redundant properties, the compiler will not throw an error.

```
let squareOptions = {colour: "red", width: 100};
let mySquare = createSquare(squareOptions);
```

Don't forget that in simple code like the one above, you probably shouldn't try to bypass this check. For more complex object literals that have methods, or that have state, you may need to use this technique, but most compiler messages related to checking for redundant properties indicate real errors. This means that when you encounter problems that such a check generates (for example, when passing an object with arguments to a function), you may need to change the type declarations. In this case, if passing an object that can have both the color and color properties is acceptable, you need to correct the SquareConfig definition to reflect this.

Functional Types

Interfaces can describe a wide range of "forms" that JS objects take. In addition to describing objects with properties, interfaces can also describe function types.

In order to describe a function using an interface, a call signature is added to it. Such a signature looks like a function description that specifies only the argument list and the return type. Each parameter in the list must have both a name and a type.

```
interface SearchFunc {
    (source: string, subString: string): boolean;
}
```

Once defined, such an interface can be used in the same way as other interfaces. Now, we will show you how to create a variable of a functional type and assign it a function.

```
let mySearch: SearchFunc;
mySearch = function(source: string, subString: string)
{
    let result = source.search(subString);
    if (result == -1) {
        return false;
    }
    else {
        return true;
    }
}
```

The parameter names do not have to match in order for the function to pass type-matching. We, for example, could write the previous example like this:

```
let mySearch: SearchFunc;
mySearch = function(src: string, sub: string): boolean
{
    let result = src.search(sub);
    if (result == -1) {
        return false;
    }
    else {
        return true;
    }
}
```

The function parameters are checked one after the other, and the parameter types that are in the corresponding positions are compared in pairs. If you don't want to specify types for arguments, then TS can infer types from the context based on the fact that the function is assigned to a variable whose type is SearchFunc. In the following example, the type of the function's return value is also output: this is done based on the values it returns (false and true). If the function returned numbers or strings, the compiler would warn during type checking that the type of the returned value does not match the type specified in the SearchFunc interface.

```
let mySearch: SearchFunc;
mySearch = function(src, sub) {
    let result = src.search(sub);
    if (result == -1) {
        return false;
    }
    else {
        return true;
    }
}
```

Indexed Types

In the same way that interfaces are used to describe functions, you can describe types so that you can use the index operator with them – for example, like this a[10] or ageMap ["daniel"]. Indexed types have an index signature that describes the types that can be used to index an object, as well as the types of values that this operation returns. Here is an example:

```
interface StringArray {
    [index: number]: string;
}

let myArray: StringArray;
myArray = ["Bob", "Josh"];

let myStr: string = myArray[0];
```

Here we have a stringArray interface that has an index signature. This signature says that when stringArray is indexed by a number, a string is returned.

There are only two types of supported index signatures: with strings and with numbers as an argument. An object can support both types, but the type of value returned by a numeric index must be a subtype of the one returned by a string index. This is because when an index operation is applied to an object, JS first converts the number passed as an index to a string. That is, using the index 100 (number) is the same as using "100" (string), so the types of both indexes must be consistent.

```
class Animal {
name: string;
}
class Dog extends Animal {
breed: string;
}
/ / Error: indexing with a string can return a Dog
object!
interface NotOkay {
[x: number]: Animal;
[x: string]: Dog;
}
```

In addition to being a powerful way to describe dictionaries, string indexes require that the types of all properties match the type that the index operation returns. This is because obj.property is also available as obj[property].

In the following example, the name type does not match the string index type, and the compiler throws an error:

```
interface NumberDictionary {
    [index: string]: number;
    length: number;      // все хорошо, length — число
    name: string;            // ошибка, the type of 'name'
is not a subtype of the indexer
}
```

In addition, the index signature can be made read-only to prevent assignment to indexes:

```
interface ReadonlyStringArray {
    readonly [index: number]: string;
}
let myArray: ReadonlyStringArray = ["Alice", "Bob"];
myArray[2] = "Mallory"; // error!
```

You can't set myArray[2] because the index signature is read-only.

INTEGRATED DEVELOPMENT ENVIRONMENTS

An integrated development environment, or simply an IDE – is a tool used to develop applications in a simple, fast, and reliable way.

In this section, we'll take a look at working with the TS environment so that you can edit, compile, run, and debug your code written in TS. TS was released as an open source project and includes both a Windows variant and a Node variant. This means that the compiler will run on Windows, Linux, macOS, and any other operating system that supports Node. In Windows environments, you can install Visual Studio, which will register *tsc.exe* (TS compiler) in our catalog c:\Program Files, or you can use Node. In Linux and macOS environments, we will need to use Node.

Node-Based Compilation

The simplest TS development environment consists of a simple text editor and a Node-based TS compiler. Go to the Node website and follow the instructions for installing Node on the operating system of your choice. Once Node is installed, you can install TS by simply typing:

```
npm install -g typescript
```

This command calls the Node Package Manager (npm) to install TS as a global module (option-g), which will make it available regardless of which directory we are currently in. After installing TS, we can display the current version of the compiler by typing the following:

```
tsc -v
```

Now let's create a TS file named *hello.ts* with the following content:

```
console.log('hello TypeScript');
```

From the command line, we can use TS to compile this file into a JS file by running the following command:

```
tsc hello.ts
```

As soon as the TS compiler finishes its work, it will generate a *hello file.js* in the current directory. We can run this file using Node by typing:

```
node hello.js
```

After that, the console will output:

```
hello TypeScript
```

Creating a *tsconfig.json* File

The TS compiler uses the tsconfig file.json in the root of the project directory to specify any global TS project parameters and compiler parameters. This means that instead of compiling our TS files one by one (specifying each file on the command line), we can simply take the tsc from the root directory of the project and TS will recursively find and compile all TS files in the root directory and in all subdirectories. The tsconfig.json file that TS needs for this can be created from the command line by simply typing:

```
tsc -init
```

The result of this command is the main tsconfig.json file:

```
{
    "compilerOptions": {
  "target": "es5",
  "module": "commonjs",
```

```
"strict": true,
"esModuleInterop": true
 }
}
```

This is a simple JSON file with a single CompilerOptions property that defines the compilation parameters for the project. The target property specifies the preferred JS output to generate, and it can be either ES3, ES5, ES6, ES2016, ES2017, or ESNext. The strict parameter is a flag that includes all parameters of strict type checking.

It is worth mentioning that TS allows you to use multiple tsconfig files. json in the catalog structure. This allows different subdirectories to use different compiler parameters.

Using our *tsconfig.json* file, we can compile our application by simply typing:

```
tsc
```

This command will call the TS compiler using the *tsconfig.json* file we created and generate the file *hello.js*. Virtually any TS source file with the extension *.ts* will generate a JS file with the *.js* extension.

Now, we have successfully created a simple TS development environment based on Node, with a simple text editor and command line access.

CHAPTER 2

Key Concepts of TS

Traditional JavaScript focuses on functions and prototype-based inheritance to develop reusable components, but this approach is quite inconvenient compared to the usual object-oriented programming, where classes inherit functionality and objects are built from these classes. Starting with ECMAScript 2015, also known as ECMAScript 6, JavaScript programmers will be able to create applications using this class-based object-oriented approach. In TypeScript (TS), you can use this approach now, and compile code in JavaScript that will work on the bulk of browsers and platforms, without waiting for the next version of JavaScript.

CLASSES

Let's look at a simple example of working with classes:

```
class Sampler {
    greeting: string;
    constructor(message: string) {
        this.greeting = message;
    }
    greet() {
        return "Hello, " + this.greeting;
    }
}

let sampler = new Sampler("world");
```

DOI: 10.1201/9781003203728-2

The syntax should be familiar if you've already programmed in C# or Java. We have declared a new Greeter class. This class has three members: the greeting property, the constructor, and the greet method.

You've noticed that when we access one of the class fields, we add this before the field name. It means that we are accessing a member of the class.

In the last line, we create an instance of the Greeter class using new. It calls the constructor that we defined earlier, creates a new object, and runs the constructor to initialize it.

Inheritance

TS uses the usual approaches of object-oriented programming. Of course, one of the most fundamental approaches in class-based programming is to create new classes using inheritance.

Inheritance is another paradigm that is one of the cornerstones of object-oriented programming. Inheritance means that an object uses another object as its base type, thereby inheriting all the characteristics of the base object, including all the properties and functions. Both interfaces and classes can use inheritance. The interface or class that inherits from it is known as the base interface or base class, and the interface or class that inherits from it is known as the derived interface or derived class. TS implements inheritance using the extends keyword.

Let's look at the following example:

```typescript
class Animal {
    name: string;
    constructor(theName: string) { this.name = theName;
}
    move(distanceInMeters: number = 0) {
        console.log('${this.name} moved
${distanceInMeters}m.');
    }
}

class Frog extends Animal {
    constructor(name: string) { super(name); }
    move(distanceInMeters = 5) {
        console.log("Jumping...");
```

```
            super.move(distanceInMeters);
        }
    }

    class Horse extends Animal {
        constructor(name: string) { super(name); }
        move(distanceInMeters = 45) {
            console.log("Galloping...");
            super.move(distanceInMeters);
        }
    }

    let jack = new Frog("Froggy the Traveller");
    let mrhorse: Animal = new Horse("MrHorse");

    jack.move();
    mrhorse.move(34);
```

This example shows the many inheritance features of TS, the same as in other languages. Here we see the *extends* keyword used to create a subclass. The Horse and Frog classes are based on the Animal class and they get access to its features.

The example shows how to override the methods of the base class using the methods that are specified in the subclass. The Frog and Horse classes create a move method that overrides the move method from the Animal class, giving it functionality specific to each of the classes. Note that although nick is declared as Animal, its value is Horse, so when nick.move(34) is called, the overridden method of the Horse class will be called.

Derived classes containing constructor functions must call super (), which will execute the constructor function of the base class.

Interface Inheritance
The following code can be an example of interface inheritance:

```
interface IBase {
    id: number | undefined;
}

interface IDerivedFromBase extends IBase {
```

```
    name: string | undefined;
}

class InterfaceInheritanceClass implements
IDerivedFromBase {
    id: number | undefined;
    name: string | undefined;
}
```

First, we have an interface called IBase, which defines the id property of the number or undefined type. Our second interface definition, IDerivedFromBase, inherits (extends) from IBase, and therefore automatically includes the id property. The IDerivedFromBase interface then defines a name property of the string or undefined type.

Since the IDerivedFromBase interface inherits from IBase, it actually has two properties – id and name. Next, we have the definition of the InterfaceInheritanceClass class, which implements the IDerivedFromBase interface. Therefore, this class must define both the id and the name property in order to successfully implement all the properties of the IDerivedFromBase interface. Although we only have the properties shown in this example, the same rules apply for functions.

Class Inheritance

Classes can also use inheritance, just like interfaces. Using our IBase and IDerivedFromBase interface definitions, the code below shows an example of class inheritance:

```
class BaseClass implements IBase {
   id: number | undefined;
}
class DerivedFromBaseClass
 extends BaseClass
 implements IDerivedFromBase {
   name: string | undefined;
}
```

The first class, BaseClass, implements the IBase interface and as such is only required to define an id property, such as number or undefined. The second class, DerivedFromBaseClass, not only inherits from the BaseClass class (using the *extends* keyword) but also implements the

IDerivedFromBase interface. Since BaseClass already defines the id property required in the IDerivedFromBase interface, the only other property that the DerivedFromBaseClass class must implement is the name property. Therefore, we need to include the definition of only this property in the DerivedFromBaseClass class.

TS does not support the concept of multiple inheritance. Multiple inheritance means that a single class can be derived from multiple base classes. TS supports only single inheritance, and therefore any class can have only one base class.

However, a class can implement many interfaces:

```
interface IFirstInterface {
    id : number | undefined;
}
interface ISecondInterface {
    name: string | undefined;
}
class MultipleInterfaces
    implements IFirstInterface, ISecondInterface {
    id: number | undefined;
    name: string | undefined;
}
```

Here we have defined two interfaces named *ifirstinterface* and *ISecondInterface*. This is followed by a class named *MultipleInterfaces*, which implements both interfaces. This means that the *MultipleInterfaces* class must implement the id property to satisfy the *IFirstInterface* interface, and the name property to satisfy the *IFirstInterface* interface.

Access Modifiers

Access modifiers allow you to hide the state of an object from external access and control access to this state. TS has three modifiers: public, protected, and private.

Public by Default

In our examples, we were able to freely access class members declared in all classes of the program. If you are familiar with classes in other languages, you may have noticed that in the examples above, we did not use the word public to change the visibility of a class member. For example,

C# requires each member to be explicitly marked public for visibility. In TS, however, each class member will be public by default.

But we can mark the members of the class public explicitly. The Animal class from the previous section will look like this:

```
class Animal {
    public name: string;
    public constructor(theName: string) { this.name =
theName; }
    public move(distanceInMeters: number) {
        console.log(`${this.name} moved
${distanceInMeters}m. `);
    }
}
```

Private Modifier

When a class member is marked with the private modifier, it cannot be accessed outside of that class. For example:

```
class Animal {
    private name: string;
    constructor(theName: string) { this.name = theName;
}
}

new Animal("Cat").name; // erroe\: 'name' is private;
```

TS is a structured type system. When we compare two different types, regardless of where and how they are described and implemented, if the types of all their members are compatible, it can be argued that the types themselves are compatible. However, when comparing types with the private access modifier, this happens differently. Two types will be considered compatible if both members have the private modifier from the same declaration. This also applies to protected members.

Let's look at an example to understand how it works in practice:

```
class Animal {
    private name: string;
    constructor(theName: string) { this.name = theName;
}
```

```
}

class Cat extends Animal {
    constructor() { super("Cat"); }
}

class Employee {
    private name: string;
    constructor(theName: string) { this.name = theName;
}
}

let animal = new Animal("Goat");
let cat = new cat();
let employee = new Employee("Jack");

animal = cat;
animal = employee; // error: 'Animal' and 'Employee'
are not compatible
```

In this example, we have the classes Animal and Cat, where Cat is a subclass of Animal. We also have a new Employee class that looks identical to Animal. We create instances of these classes and try to access each one to see what happens. Since the private part of Animal and Cat is declared in the same declaration, they are compatible. However, this does not apply to Employee. When we try to assign Employee to Animal, we get an error: these types are not compatible. Even though Employee has a private member named name, this is not the member we declared in Animal.

Protected Modifier

The protected modifier acts similarly to private, except that members declared by protected can be accessed in subclasses. For example:

```
class Person {
    protected name: string;
    constructor(name: string) { this.name = name; }
}
class Employee extends Person {
    private department: string;

    constructor(name: string, department: string) {
        super(name);
```

```
        this.department = department;
    }
    public getElevatorPitch() {
        return 'Hello, my name is ${this.name} and I
work in ${this.department}.';
    }
}
let howard = new Employee("Howard", "Sales");
console.log(howard.getElevatorPitch());
console.log(howard.name); // error
```

Note that we can't use the name member outside of the Person class, but we can use it inside the Employee subclass method, because Employee comes from Person.

The constructor can also have the protected modifier. This means that a class cannot be created outside of the class that contains it, but it can be inherited. For example:

```
class Person {
    protected name: string;
    protected constructor(theName: string) { this.
name = theName; }
}

// Employee can extend Person
class Employee extends Person {
    private department: string;

    constructor(name: string, department: string) {
        super(name);
        this.department = department;
    }

    public getElevatorPitch() {
        return `Hello, my name is ${this.name} and I
work in ${this.department}.`;
    }
}

let howard = new Employee("Howard", "Sales");
let john = new Person("John"); // error: The 'Person'
constructor is protected
```

Readonly Modifier

You can make properties read-only by using the readonly keyword. Readonly properties must be initialized when they are declared or in the constructor.

```
Class Octopus {
    readonly name: string;
    readonly numberOfLegs: number = 8;
    constructor (theName: string) {
        this.name = theName;
    }
}
let dad = new Octopus("Man with the 8 strong legs");
dad.name = "Man with the 3-piece suit"; // error! name
is readonly.
```

Type Iterator Modifier

By using the optional + sign along with the *type modifiers*, we can create more explicit and readable type declarations. We can also use the - (minus) sign to remove optional declarations from the? properties.

For example: we have an interface; we can use type iterator modifiers to make all its properties available to readonly.

```
interface ICar {
  name: string;
  age: number;
}
type ReadonlyCar = {
  readonly [K in keyof ICar]: ICar[K];
};
```

This type can be useful, for example, for the state of the Redux application because the state must be immutable.

We should not be able to change any of its properties once the object has been created. Type iterator modifiers have become a great addition to the language, as they make it easy to extend existing types and apply massive changes to all their properties.

Now, if we declare two models of the car machine: the first object is mutable, the other is readonly; then try to change their data, we will notice that in the second case we will have an error.

```
const car: ICar = {
  name: "Mercedes",
```

```
    age: 2
};
const readOnlyCar: ReadonlyCar = {
    name: "BMW",
    age: 5
};

car.age = 8;
readOnlyCar.age = 10; // Cannot assign to 'age'
because it is a read-only property
```

In the case of *ReadonlyCar.age*, TS tells us that age is *readonly – Cannot assign to 'age' because it is a read-only property.*

And this is normal, because we have specified that all its properties are readonly. The readonly status is not the only thing we can change in the type iterator modifiers.

We can specify that all properties are optional via?.

```
type ReadonlyCar = {
    readonly [K in keyof ICar]?: ICar[K];
};
```

Also, we can specify that all properties are strings, or make each property as a union of their original type and string through a vertical bar |. There are many options.

```
type ReadonlyCar = {
    readonly [K in keyof ICar]?: ICar[K] | string;
};
```

However, with the syntax readonly [K in keyof ICar]: ICar[K]; we can only add new elements to existing types. We can add the flag readonly or? sign.

If the original type has a property that is optional, for example:

```
interface ICar {
    name: string;
    age: number;
    color?: string;
}
```

We can remove the flag not only with? sign. Starting with TS 2.8, it became possible to add a minus sign (-) before the character that we want to remove.

```
type ReadonlyCar = {
  readonly [K in keyof ICar]-?: ICar[K];
};
```

As soon as we added the minus sign, TS immediately started throwing an error in const *ReadonlyCar*. This is because we suddenly missed a required property in this new object. As soon as we add a new *color* field, the error disappears.

```
const readOnlyCar: ReadonlyCar = {
  name: "BMW",
  age: 5,
  color: "black"
};
```

Since we have the flexibility with the - sign to remove flags from our types, the + sign has also been added to this feature. We can say more clearly what we are adding and what we are removing.

```
type ReadonlyCar = {
  +readonly [K in keyof ICar]-?: ICar[K];
};
```

Now everyone is reading this type, and it became clearer that we take the original ICar interface, remove all optional modifiers -? and add the +readonly flag for all properties.

Type iterator modifiers are useful if:

- there is an interface that cannot be changed directly (for example, from the library);

- there is an interface that we want to continue using for some purposes, and create a small variation of it (using modifiers) for use for other purposes;

- in both cases, the type iterator modifiers "follow" the form of the original interface; even if the original interface changes/is changed in the future, they will simply extend it according to the specified rules.

Parameter Properties

In our last example, we declared the readonly member name and the constructor parameter theName in the Octopus class, and assigned theName to name. This is a very common practice. The *parameter properties* allow you to create and initialize members in one place. Here is a further refinement of the previous Octopus class, using the parameter property:

```
class Octopus {
    readonly numberOfLegs: number = 8;
    constructor(readonly name: string) {
    }
}
```

Note how we removed theName and shortened the readonly name: string constructor parameter to create and initialize the name member. We combined the declaration and assignment in one place.

Parameter properties are declared before a constructor parameter that has an availability modifier, readonly, or both. Using the private parameter property declares and initializes the private member; so do public, protected, and readonly.

Accessors (Getters/Setters)

TS supports getters and setters as a way to intercept accesses to object properties. This gives you more control over the moment you interact with the properties of objects.

Let's rewrite a simple class using get and set. First, let's write down an example without using getters and setters.

```
class Employee {
    fullName: string;
}

let employee = new Employee();
employee.fullName = "Bob Nylon";
if (employee.fullName) {
    console.log(employee.fullName);
}
```

Allowing fullName to be set directly is quite convenient, but it can lead to problems if someone wants to change the name at will.

In this version, we check whether the user has a secret password before allowing them to make changes. We do this by replacing direct access to fullName and using the setter set, which checks the password. In addition, we add the appropriate get so that the code works the same as in the previous example.

```
let passcode = "secret passcode";

class Employee {
    private _fullName: string;

    get fullName(): string {
        return this._fullName;
    }

    set fullName(newName: string) {
        if (passcode && passcode == "secret passcode")
{
            this._fullName = newName;
        }
        else {
            console.log("Error: Unauthorized update of
employee!");
        }
    }
}

let employee = new Employee();
employee.fullName = "Bob Nylon";
if (employee.fullName) {
    console.log(employee.fullName);
}
```

To make sure that our access method checks the password, we can modify it and see that if there is a mismatch, we get a message that we can't modify the worker object.

Attention: accessors require the installation of code generation in the compiler according to the ECMAScript 5 standard or higher.

Static Properties
So far, we've only talked about class instance members, the ones that appear in an object when it's initialized. But we can also create static class

members, those that are visible in the class without creating an instance. In this example, we use *static*, since *origin* is a common value for all objects. Each instance accesses this value by prefixing it with the class name. Similar to how we add *this.* to access instance members, the *Grid* is used to access static members.

```
class Grid {
    static origin = {x: 0, y: 0};
    calculateDistanceFromOrigin(point: {x: number; y:
number;}) {
        let xDist = (point.x - Grid.origin.x);
        let yDist = (point.y - Grid.origin.y);
        return Math.sqrt(xDist * xDist + yDist *
yDist) / this.scale;
    }
    constructor (public scale: number) { }
}

let grid1 = new Grid(1.0);   // 1x scale
let grid2 = new Grid(5.0);   // 5x scale

console.log(grid1.calculateDistanceFromOrigin({x: 10,
y: 10}));
console.log(grid2.calculateDistanceFromOrigin({x: 10,
y: 10}));
```

Abstract Classes

Abstract classes are base classes from which others inherit. Their instances cannot be created directly. Unlike an interface, an abstract class can contain the implementation details of its members. The abstract keyword is used to define abstract classes, as well as abstract methods within such classes.

```
abstract class Animal {
    abstract makeSound(): void;
    move(): void {
        console.log("doing something...");
    }
}
```

Methods within an abstract class that are marked as abstract do not contain an implementation and must be implemented in derived classes. Abstract methods have the same syntax as interface methods. Both define the signature of a method without describing its body. The abstract method description must contain the abstract keyword, and can also contain access modifiers.

```
abstract class Department {
    constructor(public name: string) {
    }
    printName(): void {
        console.log("Department name: " + this.name);
    }
    abstract printMeeting(): void; // must be
implemented in a derived class
}

class AccountingDepartment extends Department {
    constructor() {
        super("Accounting and Auditing"); //
constructors in derived classes must call
super()
    }
    printMeeting(): void {
        console.log("The Accounting Department meets
each Monday at 10am.");
    }
    generateReports(): void {
        console.log("Generating accounting
reports...");
    }
}
let department: Department; // okaycreated a reference
to an abstract class
department = new Department(); // error: cannot create
an instance of an abstract class
department = new AccountingDepartment(); // okay, a
non-abstract class was created and assigneddepartment.
printName();
department.printMeeting();
department.generateReports(); // error: method doesn't
exist on declared abstract type
```

Constructors

When you declare a class in TS, you are actually creating multiple declarations at the same time. The first declaration is of the class instance type.

```
class Greeter {
    greeting: string;
    constructor(message: string) {
        this.greeting = message;
    }
    greet() {
        return "Hello, " + this.greeting;
    }
}
let greeter: Greeter;
greeter = new Greeter("world");
console.log(greeter.greet());
```

In this case, when we say let greeter: Greeter, we use Greeter as the type of instances of the Greeter class. This is almost a habit of programmers from other object-oriented programming languages.

We also create another value, which is called a constructor function. This function is called when we create instances of the class using new. To see how this looks in practice, let's look at the JavaScript code generated by the compiler from the example above:

```
let Greeter = (function () {
    function Greeter(message) {
        this.greeting = message;
    }
    Greeter.prototype.greet = function () {
        return "Hello, " + this.greeting;
    };
    return Greeter;
})();

let greeter;
greeter = new Greeter("world");
console.log(greeter.greet());
```

Here let Greeter is assigned a constructor function. When we specify new and run this function, we get an instance of the class. The constructor function also contains all the static members of the class. Another way to think about each class is: there is an instance part and a static part.

Let's change the code a bit to show this difference:

```
class Greeter {
    static standardGreeting = "Hello, there";
```

```
greeting: string;
greet() {
    if (this.greeting) {
        return "Hello, " + this.greeting;
    }
    else {
        return Greeter.standardGreeting;
    }
}
}
let greeter1: Greeter;
greeter1 = new Greeter();
console.log(greeter1.greet());

let greeterMaker: typeof Greeter = Greeter;
greeterMaker.standardGreeting = "Hey there!";

let greeter2: Greeter = new greeterMaker();
console.log(greeter2.greet());
```

In this example, greeter1 works similarly to the one above. We created an instance of the Greeter class and use the object. We have already seen this.

Then we use the class directly. Creating a new variable named greeterMaker. This variable will contain the class itself, or, in other words, the constructor function. Here we use typeof Greeter, it looks like "give me the type of the Greeter class itself," not the instance. Or, more precisely, "give me an ID type called Greeter," which is the type of the constructor function. This type will contain all the static members of Greeter, along with a constructor that creates instances of the Greeter class. We demonstrated this by using new with greeterMaker, creating new instances of Greeter and calling them as before.

Using a Class as an Interface

As we discussed in the previous section, a class declaration creates two things: a type that describes instances of the class, and a constructor function. Since classes create types, we can use them in the same way as interfaces.

```
class Point {
    x: number;
    y: number;
}
```

```
interface Point3d extends Point {
    z: number;
}

let point3d: Point3d = {x: 1, y: 2, z: 3};
```

FUNCTIONS

Functions are one of the fundamental foundations of any JavaScript application. They are used to build abstraction levels, classes, information hiding, and modules. TS has classes, namespaces, and modules, but functions play a key role. The TS language slightly expands the capabilities of functions compared to JavaScript, making working with them even more convenient.

As in JavaScript, functions in TS can be either named or anonymous. This allows you to choose the most convenient approach for developing your application, whether it is building a list of functions in the API, or embedding one function in another.

Let's recall how these two options look in JavaScript:

```
// Named function
function add (x, y) {
return x + y;
}
/ / Anonymous function
let myAdd = function(x, y) {return x+y; };
```

Just like in JavaScript, functions can access variables outside of their body. When this happens, the function is said to "capture" the variables. Although it is not the task of this article to explain how it works and what the pitfalls of this technique are, it is important to have a clear understanding of this mechanism in order to work with JavaScript and TS.

```
let z = 50;

function addToZ(x, y) {
    return x + y + z;
}
```

Types of Functions
Adding Types to a Function
Let's add the types to the function from the previous simple examples:

```
function add(x: number, y: number): number {
    return x + y;
```

```
}
let myAdd = function(x: number, y: number): number
{return x+y; };
```

You can add types to each parameter, as well as to the function itself, to specify the type of the return value. TS can infer the type of the return value itself by analyzing the return statements, so it is often possible not to specify it explicitly.

Now let's describe the full type of this function:

```
let myAdd: (x: number, y: number)=>number =
    function(x: number, y: number): number {return
x+y; };
```

A functional type consists of two parts: the argument types and the return type. The type of the return value is determined after =>. In the event that the function does not return any value, void must be specified.

Also in the example above, we changed the names of the parameters passed to the function. This is done for better code readability. You should always try to give "talking" or understandable names to the parameters. This will make it easier for others to read your code, as well as for you when you return to it after some time.

It is worth noting that only the parameters passed to the function and the return value determine its type. The captured variables are not included in the type description. Therefore, they are part of a certain "hidden state" of the function and are not included in the API.

Inferring Types

Experimenting with the following example, you can see that the TS compiler is able to deal with types if they are specified in only one-half of the expression:

```
// myAdd has the full function type
let myAdd = function(x: number, y: number): number {
return   x + y; };
// Parameters 'x' and 'y' — has "number" type
let myAdd: (baseValue:number, increment:number) =>
number =
    function(x, y) { return x + y; };
```

This is called contextual typing – a type inference. This feature allows you to spend less effort on adding types to the program.

There are several places in TS where type inference is used to get information about types without explicitly specifying it. For example, in this code

```
let x = 3;
```

The type of the variable x is output in number. This kind of inference occurs when initializing variables and members, assigning default values to parameters, and defining the type of the function's return value.

In most cases, type inference is fairly straightforward. In the following sections, we will describe several subtleties of this process.

Best General Type

When inference is made from multiple expressions, their types are used to find the "best general type." For example,

```
let x = [0, 1, null];
```

To output the type x in this case, you need to check the type of each element in the array. In this case, there are two options for the array type: number and null. The algorithm for finding the best common type checks each candidate type, and selects the one that is compatible with all the others.

Since the best common type must be chosen from the types provided, there are cases where the types have a common structure for all, but none of them is the base for all the others. For example:

```
let zoo = [new Rhino(), new Elephant(), new Snake()];
```

Ideally, we would like the zoo type to be output as Animal[] (that is, an array of objects of the Animal – animal class). But, since there is not a single object in the array that has the Animal class, the compiler is not able to get such a result. To fix this, you will have to explicitly specify the type if no object has the base type for all the others:

```
let zoo: Animal[] = [new Rhino(), new Elephant(), new Snake()];
```

If the compiler cannot find the best common type, the output will be the type of an empty object, that is, {}. Since this type has no members, attempting to use any of its properties will result in an error. As a result of this inference, you can still use the object as if its type is unknown, and guarantee type safety in cases where the object type cannot be found implicitly.

Context Type

In some cases, type inference works in the "other direction" as well. This is called "context typing." Contextual typing occurs when you can make a guess about the type of an expression based on its position. For example:

```
window.onmousedown = function(mouseEvent) {
    console.log(mouseEvent.button); //<- Error
};
```

To find the type error in this example, the compiler first used the Window. onmousedown function type to infer the type of the function expression from the right side of the assignment. After that, it was able to output the type of the MouseEvent parameter. If this function expression was located where its type could not be inferred from the context, the type of the MouseEvent parameter would be any, and the compiler would not throw an error.

If an expression whose type was inferred from the context contains an explicit type indication, the inferred context type is ignored. That is, if the previous example were written as:

```
window.onmousedown = function(MouseEvent: any) {
console. log(MouseEvent.buton); / / < - No error is
shown now
};
```

The explicitly specified parameter type in the function expression will take precedence over the context type. For this reason, the compiler will not throw an error, since the context type is not applied.

Contextual typing is used in many cases. Typically, these are arguments when calling functions, the right-hand side of an assignment, type checks, object members and array literals, and return statements.

Also, the context type is used as a candidate for the best general type. For example:

```
function createZoo(): Animal[] {
    return [new Rhino(), new Elephant(), new Snake()];
}
```

There are four candidates for the best overall type: Animal, Rhino, Elephant, and Snake. The algorithm for finding the best general type is able to choose Animal from them.

Anonymous Functions

JavaScript also has the concept of anonymous functions. These are functions that are defined during the operation and do not specify a function name. Consider the JavaScript code below:

```
var addVar = function(a,b) {
  return a + b;
}
var addVarResult = addVar(2,3);
console.log("addVarResult:"" + addVarResult);
```

Here, we define a function that has no name and adds two values. Since the function has no name, it is known as an anonymous function. This anonymous function is then assigned to a variable named addVar. The addVar variable can be called as a function with two parameters, and the return value will be the result of executing an anonymous function. The output of this code will be as follows:

```
addVarResult:5
```

Let's now rewrite the previous anonymous JavaScript function in TS:

```
var addFunction = function(a:number, b:number) :
number {
    return a + b;
}
var addFunctionResult = addFunction(2,3);
console.log('addFunctionResult :
${addFunctionResult}');
```

Here, you can see that TS allows anonymous functions in the same way as JavaScript, but still allows standard type annotations. The result of this code is as follows:

```
addFunctionResult: 5
```

Type Compatibility

Type compatibility in TS is based on structural typing. Structural typing is a way to identify type relationships based solely on the composition of their members. This approach differs from nominative typing. Let's look at the following code:

```
interface Named {
name: string;
}

class Person {
name: string;
}

let p: Named;
// Everything fits, since the structural type system
p = new Person is used();
```

In languages like C# and Java, where the nominative type system is used, similar code would lead to an error, since the Person class is not explicitly described as implementing the Named interface.

The TS structural type system was designed with the way JavaScript code is usually written in mind. Since JavaScript makes extensive use of anonymous objects, such as function expressions and object literals, it is much more natural to describe their relationships using a structural system rather than a nominative one.

The TS type system allows for certain operations that cannot be said to be safe at compile time. When a type system has this property, it is said that it is not "reliable." The places where TS allows unreliable behavior have been carefully considered, and in this chapter, we will explain where this happens and for what reason it was allowed.

The basic rule of the TS type system is that x is compatible with y if y has at least the same members as x. For example:

```
interface with the name {
name: string;
}
```

```
let x: Named;
// the output type for y is {name: string; location:
string;}
let y = {name: "Jannet", location: "Boston"};
x = y;
```

To understand whether y can be assigned to x, the compiler searches for the corresponding compatible property in y for each of the properties of x. In this case, the y variable must have a property named name of the string type. It is there, and assignment is allowed.

The same rule is used in the case of checking arguments when calling a function:

```
function greeting (n: By name) {
alert ("Hello," + n.name);
}
greet(y); / / OK
```

Note that y has an additional location property, but this does not result in an error. When checking for compatibility, only members of the target type (in this case, Named) are considered.

The comparison process is performed recursively, affecting the types of all members and sub-members.

Optional Parameters and Default Parameters
In TS, it is assumed that each function parameter is required. This does not mean that it cannot be passed *null* or *undefined*: it means that when the function is called, the compiler will check whether the user has set a value for each of its parameters. In addition, the compiler assumes that no parameters other than those specified will be passed. Simply put, the number of parameters passed must match the number of parameters that the function expects.

```
function buildName(firstName: string, lastName:
string) {
return firstName + "" + lastName;
}

let result1 = buildName("Sam"); // error, too few
parameters
```

```
let result2 = buildName("Sam", "Adams", "Sr."); //
error, too many parameters
let result3 = buildName("Sam", "Adams"); // correct
```

In JavaScript, all parameters are optional, and users can skip them if necessary. In such cases, the value of the missing parameters is assumed to be *undefined*. In TS, you can also achieve this: to do this, at the end of the parameter that you want to make optional,? is added. For example, we want to make *lastName* optional from the previous example:

```
function buildName(firstName: string, lastName?:
string) {
    if (lastName)
        return firstName + " " + lastName;
    else
        return firstName;
}

let result1 = buildName("Sam");          // all is
correct now
let result2 = buildName("Sam", "Adams", "Sr.");  //
error, too many parameters
let result3 = buildName("Sam", "Adams");          //
correct
```

All optional parameters must come after the required ones. If the first parameter (firstName) had to be made optional instead of *lastName*, then the order of the parameters in the function would have to be changed so that *firstName* would be the last.

TS also allows you to specify a value for a parameter that it will accept if the user skips it or passes *undefined*. These parameters are called default parameters, or simply default parameters. Let's take the previous example and set the default value for *lastName* to "Smith."

```
function buildName(firstName: string, lastName =
"Smith") {
    return firstName + " " + lastName;
}

let result1 = buildName("Sam");                // now
all is correct, returns "Sam Smith"
```

```
let result2 = buildName("Sam", undefined);          // also
works and returns "Sam Smith"
let result3 = buildName("Sam", "Adams", "Sr.");    //
error, too many parameters
let result4 = buildName("Sam", "Adams");            //
correct
```

The default parameters that follow all the required parameters are considered optional. Just like the optional ones, you can skip them when calling the function. This means that the types of optional parameters and default parameters that are at the end will be compatible, so this function …

```
function buildName(firstName: string, lastName?:
string) {
    // …
}
```

And this

```
function buildName(firstName: string, lastName =
"Smith") {
    // …
}
```

will have the same type (firstName: string, lastName?: string) = > string. The default value for the *lastName* parameter in the function type description disappears, leaving only the fact that the last parameter is optional.

Unlike simple optional parameters, the default parameters do not have to be placed after the required parameters. If the default parameter is followed by a mandatory parameter, you will have to explicitly pass undefined to set the default value. For example, the last example can be rewritten using only the default parameter for *firstName*:

```
function buildName(firstName = "Will", lastName:
string) {
    return firstName + " " + lastName;
}

let result1 = buildName("Sam");                     //
error, too few parameters
```

```
let result2 = buildName("Sam", "Adams", "Sr.");   //
error, too many parameters
let result3 = buildName("Sam", "Adams");          //
works and returns "Bob Adams"
let result4 = buildName(undefined, "Adams");      //
works and returns "Will Adams"
```

Rest Parameters

Mandatory, optional, and default parameters have one thing in common – they describe one parameter at a time. In some cases, you need to work with several parameters, treating them as a group; and sometimes it is not known in advance how many parameters the function will take. In JavaScript, you can work with arguments directly using the arguments variable, which is available inside any function.

In TS, you can assemble arguments into a single variable:

```
function buildName(firstName: string, ...restOfName:
string[]) {
    return firstName + " " + restOfName.join(" ");
}

let employeeName = buildName("Jonas", "Pitt", "Lucas",
"Samuel");
```

Rest parameters can be understood as an unlimited number of optional parameters. When passing arguments for residual parameters, you can pass as many of them as you want; or you can pass nothing at all. The compiler will build an array from the passed arguments, assign it a name that is specified after the ellipsis (...), and make it available inside the function.

The ellipsis is also used when describing the type of function with residual parameters:

```
function buildName(firstName: string, ...restOfName:
string[]) {
    return firstName + " " + restOfName.join(" ");
}

let buildNameFun: (fname: string, ...rest: string[])
=> string = buildName;
```

this Keyword

Learning how to use *this* keyword correctly in JavaScript is something of a rite of passage for developers. Since TS is a superset of JavaScript, TS programmers also need to understand how to use *this* and how to notice when this is used incorrectly. Fortunately, TS allows you to detect the incorrect use of *this* with a few tricks.

As a rule, an object method needs access to the information stored in the object in order to perform any actions with it (in accordance with the purpose of the method).

For example, the code inside *user. SayHi()* may need the user name that is stored in the *user* object. To access information inside an object, a method can use the *this* keyword. The value of this is the "before the dot" object that was used to call the method.

```
let user = {
name: "John",
age: 30,

SayHi() {
// this is the " current object"
alert(this.name);
}

};

user.SayHi (); / / John
```

Here, during the execution of the *user.SayHi ()* code, the value of this will be user (a reference to the user object).

Technically, it is also possible to access an object without the *this* keyword by referring to it through an external variable (which stores a reference to this object):

```
let user = {
name: "John",
age: 30,

SayHi() {
alert(user.name); / / use the "user" variable instead
of the "this" keyword"
}
};
```

But such code will be unreliable. If we decide to copy the reference to the user object to another variable, for example, admin = user, and overwrite the user variable with something else, then the wrong object will be accessed when calling the method from admin.

This is shown below:

```
let user = {
name: "John",
age: 30,
SayHi() {
alert( user.name ); / / will result in an error
}

};

let admin = user;
user = null; // reset the variable for clarity, now it
does not store a reference to the object.

admin.SayHi (); / / Error! Inside SayHi (), the user
is used, which no longer references the object!
```

If we use this.name instead of user.name inside the alert, then this code will work.

Keyword "this" and Arrow Functions

The keyword *this* is a variable that is set when the function is called. This is a very powerful and flexible feature of the language, but in return for its advantages, you always have to remember the context in which the function is executed. It's easy to get confused here, especially when a function is returned as a result or passed as an argument.

Let's look at an example:

```
let deck = {
    suits: ["hearts", "spades", "clubs", "diamonds"],
    cards: Array(52),
    createCardPicker: function() {
        return function() {
            let pickedCard = Math.floor(Math.random()
* 52);
            let pickedSuit = Math.floor(pickedCard /
13);
```

```
        return {suit: this.suits[pickedSuit],
card: pickedCard % 13};
        }
    }
}

let cardPicker = deck.createCardPicker();
let pickedCard = cardPicker();

alert("card: " + pickedCard.card + " of " +
pickedCard.suit);
```

Note that createCardPicker is a function that returns a function. If we try
to run this example, we will get an error instead of the expected message.
This is because this, which is used in the function created by createCard-
Picker, points to the window and not to the deck object. All this is due to
the fact that cardPicker() is called by itself. When using a similar syntax,
when a function is called as a non-method, and at the very top level of the
program, this will point to window. (Note: in strict mode, in such cases,
this will have the value undefined, not window.)

You can fix this by making sure that the function is bound to the correct
value of this before returning it. In this case, regardless of how it will be
used in the future, it will still have access to the original deck object. To do
this, you need to change the function, and use the syntax of the arrow function from the ECMAScript 6 standard. Arrow functions capture the value
of this as it was at the time of its creation (and not at the time of the call):

```
let deck = {
    suits: ["hearts", "spades", "clubs", "diamonds"],
    cards: Array(52),
    createCardPicker: function() {
    //ATTENTION: the line below is an arrow
function that captures the value of 'this' from this
place
        return () => {
            let pickedCard = Math.floor(Math.random()
* 52);
            let pickedSuit = Math.floor(pickedCard /
13);
            return {suit: this.suits[pickedSuit],
card: pickedCard % 13};
```

```
        }
      }
}
```

```
let cardPicker = deck.createCardPicker();
let pickedCard = cardPicker();

alert("card: " + pickedCard.card + " of " +
pickedCar8d.suit);
```

Even better, if you pass the *-noImplicitThis* flag to the compiler, TS will issue a warning if you make a similar error. It will indicate that this in the expression *this. suits[pickedSuit]* is of type any.

this Parameters

Unfortunately, the type of the expression *this. suits[pickedSuit]* is still any, since this is taken from a function expression inside an object literal. To fix this, you can explicitly specify this as a parameter. The *this* parameter is a "fake" parameter that comes first in the list of function parameters:

```
function f(this: void) {
// Ensure that 'this' cannot be used in this separate
function
}
```

We will add several interfaces to the previous example: Card and Deck, to make the types more understandable and easy to reuse:

```
interface Card {
    suit: string;
    card: number;
}
interface Deck {
    suits: string[];
    cards: number[];
    createCardPicker(this: Deck): () => Card;
}
let deck: Deck = {
    suits: ["hearts", "spades", "clubs", "diamonds"],
    cards: Array(52),
    // ATTENTION: Now the function explicitly
indicates that it should be called on an object of the
Deck type
```

```
    createCardPicker: function(this: Deck) {
        return () => {
            let pickedCard = Math.floor(Math.random()
* 52);
            let pickedSuit = Math.floor(pickedCard /
13);
            return {suit: this.suits[pickedSuit],
card: pickedCard % 13};
        }
    }
}

let cardPicker = deck.createCardPicker();
let pickedCard = cardPicker();
alert("card: " + pickedCard.card + " of " +
pickedCard.suit);
```

The compiler now knows that the *createCardPicker* function expects to be called on an object with the Deck type. This means that the type of this value is now Deck, not any, and the *–noImplicitThis* flag will not throw errors.

this Parameters for Callback Functions

You may also encounter this-related errors in callback functions when the functions are passed to a library that will later call them. Since the passed function will be called by the library as a normal function, this will have the value undefined. With some effort, you can use the *this* parameter to prevent such errors. First, the library developer must accompany the type of the callback function with the *this* parameter:

```
interface UIElement {
    addClickListener(onclick: (this: void, e: Event) =>
void): void;
}
```

this: void means that *addClickListener* assumes that the onclick function does not require this. Secondly, the code that is called must also be accompanied by the *this* parameter:

```
class Handler {
    info: string;
    onClickBad(this: Handler, e: Event) {
```

```
        // this is used here! The function will crash
at runtime!
        this.info = e.message;
    };
}
let h = new Handler();
uiElement.addClickListener(h.onClickBad); // error!
```

When this is specified, it explicitly reflects the fact that *onClickBad* must be called on an instance of the Handler class. Now TS will detect that addClickListener requires a function with *this: void*. To fix this error, change the *this* type:

```
class Handler {
    info: string;
    onClickGood(this: void, e: Event) {
        // you can't use the this variable here,
because it has the void type!
        console.log('clicked!');
    }
}
let h = new Handler();
uiElement.addClickListener(h.onClickGood);
```

Since the *onClickGood* function specifies that the type of this is void, it can be passed to *addClickListener*. Of course, this also means that it can no longer be used in it *this.info*. But if you need both, you will have to use the arrow function:

```
class Handler {
    info: string;
    onClickGood = (e: Event) => {this.info = e.message}
}
```

This will work because arrow functions do not capture this from the context in which they are executed, and they can be freely passed where a function with *this: void* is expected. The disadvantage of this solution is that for each Handler object, its own arrow function will be created. Methods, on the other hand, are created only once, are associated with the Handler prototype, and are common to all objects of this class.

Overloads

TS supports function overloading, meaning we can define multiple versions of a function that will have the same name, but different parameter types or different number of parameters. For overloading, we first define all versions of the function that will not have any logic. And then we define a version of the function with a common signature that fits all the previously defined options. And in this general version, we already define the specific logic of the function.

For example, we need to combine two values, but if they represent strings, then just concatenate them, and if numbers, then add them. Then we could use the following function:

```
function add(x: string, y: string): string;
function add(x: number, y: number): number;
function add(x: any, y: any): any {
    return x + y;
}
```

```
let result1 = add(5, 7);
console.log(result1);    // 12
let result2 = add("5", "7");
console.log(result2);    // 57
```

The first version of the add function takes two strings and returns a string, the second version takes two numbers and returns a number. Common to them is a function that takes parameters of type any and returns a result of type any as well.

But if we applied the same function to *boolean* values:

```
let result3 = add(true, false);
console.log(result3);
```

Then we would get an error, since two versions of the function allow you to take either two strings or two numbers as parameters. And in this case, we would need to add another version of the function for *boolean* values:

```
function add(x: boolean, y: boolean): boolean;
```

JavaScript is by its very nature a very dynamic language. It is not uncommon to find functions that return objects of different types depending on the arguments passed.

```
let suits = ["hearts", "spades", "clubs", "diamonds"];

function pickCard(x): any {
    // Working with object/array?
    // So, we were given a deck and we choose a card
    if (typeof x == "object") {
        let pickedCard = Math.floor(Math.random() *
x.length);
        return pickedCard;
    }
    // Otherwise, we give you the opportunity to
choose a card
    else if (typeof x == "number") {
        let pickedSuit = Math.floor(x / 13);
        return { suit: suits[pickedSuit], card: x % 13
};
    }
}

let myDeck = [{ suit: "diamonds", card: 2 }, { suit:
"spades", card: 10 }, { suit: "hearts", card: 4 }];
let pickedCard1 = myDeck[pickCard(myDeck)];
alert("card: " + pickedCard1.card + " of " +
pickedCard1.suit);

let pickedCard2 = pickCard(15);
alert("card: " + pickedCard2.card + " of " +
pickedCard2.suit);
```

In this example, the pickCard function returns two different things, depending on what was passed to it. If the user has passed an object that represents a deck of cards, the function will select one of the cards. If the user passes the card, the function will determine which card he chose. But how do you describe this behavior using a type system?

You need to specify several types for one function, creating a list of overloads. The compiler will use this list for checks when calling the function. Let's create a list of overloads that describes what the *pickCard* function accepts and what it returns.

```
let suits = ["hearts", "spades", "clubs", "diamonds"];

function pickCard(x: {suit: string; card: number; }
[]): number;
```

```
function pickCard(x: number): {suit: string; card:
number; };
function pickCard(x): any {
    // Working with object/array?
    // So, we were given a deck and we choose a card
    if (typeof x == "object") {
        let pickedCard = Math.floor(Math.random() *
x.length);
        return pickedCard;
    }
    // Otherwise, we give you the opportunity to
choose a card
    else if (typeof x == "number") {
        let pickedSuit = Math.floor(x / 13);
        return { suit: suits[pickedSuit], card: x %
13 };
    }
}

let myDeck = [{ suit: "diamonds", card: 2 }, { suit:
"spades", card: 10 }, { suit: "hearts", card: 4 }];
let pickedCard1 = myDeck[pickCard(myDeck)];
alert("card: " + pickedCard1.card + " of " +
pickedCard1.suit);

let pickedCard2 = pickCard(15);
alert("card: " + pickedCard2.card + " of " +
pickedCard2.suit);
```

By changing the code in this way, we get the ability to call the pickCard function, performing a type check.

In order to select the correct type check, the compiler performs actions similar to those in JavaScript. It looks through the list of overloads, starting with the first element, and matches the function parameters. If the parameters are appropriate, the compiler selects this overload as the correct one. Therefore, as a rule, function overloads are ordered from the most specific to the least specific.

Note that the code section function *pickCard(x): any* is not included in the list of overloads; there are only two elements in this list, one of which takes an object and the other a number. Calling *pickCard* with any other types of parameters will result in an error.

GENERICS

One of the most important aspects of software development is the creation of components with a well-designed structure and API. But an equally important part is the ability to reuse these components. Components that can work with different data sets provide developers with additional capabilities when designing large and complex systems.

In languages such as Java or C#, one of the main ways to create reusable components is to use generics. Generalizations allow the component to work with different types of data, depending on the needs of developers.

Exploring the World of Generics

To begin with, we will create the first function that is traditional for acquaintance with generalizations: the identity function. Such a function returns exactly what was passed to it. You can think of it the same way as the echo command.

```
function identity(arg: number): number {
    return arg;
}
```

Of course, in TS, we can specify any so that the function can be used for any data type:

```
function identity(arg: any): any {
    return arg;
}
```

We can say that this function is a generalization, since it can work with any type of data. But in this case, we have absolutely no information about the type of the returned value. For example, we pass a number as an arg, but we don't know anything about the specific type that the function will return, since it is any.

When using generalizations, we can explicitly specify the type of the argument and thus, within the framework of our example, determine the type of the return value. To do this, we need to use a special type variable that only works with data types, not their values:

```
function identity<t>(arg: T): T {
    return arg;
}
</t>
```

We added a variable of type T to our function. This variable allows us to specify a specific type when using the function. In addition, we also specified the type of the return value. And now we know that the function will return the result with the same data type as the passed argument.

Now let's see how you can use our function. There are two ways to do this. Consider the first one:

```
let numberOutput = identity<Number>(1);
let wrongOutput = identity<Number>("sdf"); / /
Compilation error. Invalid data type for the argument
let stringOutput = identity<String>("String");

console. log(numberOutput); / / outputs "1"
console. log (stringOutput); / / outputs " String"
```

When calling the function in angle brackets < >, we explicitly specified the data type that the function will work with.

The second method is not to specify the data type in angle brackets, but simply pass the variable as an argument to the function. In this case, TS uses a mechanism called automatic type inference, according to the value passed as an argument.

```
let numberOutput = identity(1);
let stringOutput = identity ("String");

console. log(numberOutput); / / outputs " 1 "
console. log (stringOutput);/ / outputs " String"
```

The second method, on the one hand, makes the code shorter and easier to read, but on the other hand, it can lead to errors. After all, in this case, you can pass a value to the function that is not expected there, and this can lead to an error at runtime.

Working with Generalized Type Variables

When using generalizations, the compiler assumes that the generalized parameters passed to the function are used correctly. In fact, the compiler treats them as "any data type" or any.

Let's look at the function from the previous section again:

```
function identity<t>(arg: T): T {
   return arg;
}
</t>
```

What if you need to output the length of the arg argument to the console every time the function is called? You may be tempted to write like this:

```
function loggingIdentity<t>(arg: T): T {
    console.log(arg.length);  // Error: T has no
.length property
    return arg;
}
</t>
```

If you do this, the compiler will throw an error telling you what is being used the *.length* of the arg object, although it was never specified that the object has such a property. Earlier it was said that a type variable means absolutely any type, so a number that does not have a property could also be passed to the function *.length*.

Let's assume that the function should actually work with arrays of T objects, and not with the T objects themselves directly. Since it will deal with arrays, they must have a property .length. You can describe it as if we are creating an array:

```
function loggingIdentity<t>(arg: T[]): T[] {
    console.log(arg.length);  // Array has .length, so
there is no error
    return arg;
}
</t>
```

The *loggingIdentity* type is read as "a generalized loggingIdentity function that takes a type parameter T and an argument arg, which is an array of objects T, and returns an array of objects T." If an array of numbers is passed to the function, the result will also be an array of numbers, since T will become number. This allows us to use the generalized type variable T as part of the type we are working with, rather than just as an entire type, which gives us more flexibility.

Alternatively, you can write this example in the following way:

```
function loggingIdentity<t>(arg: Array<t>): Array<t> {
    console.log(arg.length);  // Array has .length, so
there is no error
    return arg;
}
</t></t></t>
```

You may have already encountered this kind of type writing in other languages. In the next section, we'll discuss how to create your own custom types like Array<T>.

Generalized Types

In the previous sections, we created a generalized identity function that worked with different types. In this section, we will discuss how to describe the type of such a function and how to create generalized interfaces.

Defining a generic function type is very similar to defining a type for a regular function. The only difference is that you first need to specify the type of parameters to be passed and the return value, just like when creating a generalized function:

```
function
 identity<t>(arg: T): T {
    return arg;
}

let myIdentity: <t>(arg: T) => T = identity;
</t></t>
```

A different name could be used for the standard parameter, but it is only important that the number of standard parameters and how they are used are consistent.

```
function identity<t>(arg: T): T {
    return arg;
}

let myIdentity: <U>(arg: U) => U = identity;
</t>
```

You can also write a generic type as a call signature on the type of an object literal:

```
function identity<t>(arg: T): T {
    return arg;
}

let myIdentity: {<t>(arg: T): T} = identity;
</t></t>
```

This brings us to the description of the first generalized interface. Let's take the object literal from the previous example and turn it into an interface:

```
interface GenericIdentityFn {
    <t>(arg: T): T;
}

function identity<t>(arg: T): T {
    return arg;
}

let myIdentity: GenericIdentityFn = identity;
</t></t>
```

Moreover, we can specify a generic type for the entire interface, which will make this parameter available to all its methods. After that, we can use a generalized version of the interface, specifying a specific data type (for example, Dictionary<string> instead of Dictionary):

```
interface GenericIdentityFn<t> {
    (arg: T): T;
}

function identity<t>(arg: T): T {
    return arg;
}

let myIdentity: GenericIdentityFn<number> = identity;
</number></t></t>
```

Note that the example was transformed into something completely different. Instead of describing a generalized function, it is now an ordinary, non-generalized function that is part of a generalized type. When using GenericIdentityFn, you will now have to specify the appropriate type argument (in this case, number), thus fixing the types that the corresponding function will use. Understanding when a type parameter should be added to the call signature and when to the interface itself is useful when describing which aspects of the type are generalized.

In addition to generic interfaces, you can also create generic classes. Note that you cannot create generic enumerations and namespaces.

Generalized Classes

Generalized classes have the same form as generalized interfaces. They have a list of typical parameters in angle brackets (< >) after the class name.

```
class GenericNumber<t> {
    zeroValue: T;
    add: (x: T, y: T) => T;
}

let myGenericNumber = new GenericNumber<number>();
myGenericNumber.zeroValue = 0;
myGenericNumber.add = function(x, y) { return x + y;
};
</number></t>
```

This is a fairly literal use of the GenericNumber type (lit. a generalized number), but you can see that nothing prevents you from using other types with it, except number. For example, you can use the string type or more complex objects.

```
let stringNumeric = new GenericNumber<string>();
stringNumeric.zeroValue = "";
stringNumeric.add = function(x, y) { return x + y; };

alert(stringNumeric.add(stringNumeric.zeroValue,
"test"));
</string>
```

Just as with interfaces, passing a type parameter to the class itself establishes that all its properties will work with the same type.

As mentioned in Chapter 2, a class has two types: the static part type and the instance type. Generic types are such only in relation to the instance type, but not to the static part type. Therefore, static class members cannot use typical class parameters.

Limitations of Generalizations

As you remember from the previous examples, in some cases you need to create a generalized function that works with a certain set of types, for which you know what capabilities they have. In the example with loggingIdentity, you needed to access the property .the length of the arg object, but the compiler couldn't be sure that any type would have such a property, so it warned about it.

```
function loggingIdentity<t>(arg: T): T {
   console.log(arg.length);   // Error: T has no
.length property
   return arg;
}
</t>
```

Instead of working with any possible type, we would like to create a constraint so that the function works with all types that have a property .length. If a type has this property, it can be used, but it must have at least this property.

To implement this, we will create an interface that describes such a restriction. Creating an interface with a single property. length, and use it with the extend keyword to denote a constraint:

```
interface Lengthwise {
   length: number;
}

function loggingIdentity<t extends=""
lengthwise="">(arg: T): T {
   console.log(arg.length);   // Now we know that the
object has a property .length, so there is no error
   return arg;
}
</t>
```

Since the generalized function now has a constraint, it will not be able to work with any type:

```
loggingIdentity(3); / / Error, the number has no
.length property
```

Instead, it needs to pass values of those types that have all the necessary properties:

```
loggingIdentity({length: 10, value: 3});
```

Using Generic Parameters in Generalization Constraints
You can define a type parameter that will be limited to the type of another type parameter. For example, we want to get a property of an object by

its name. And we really don't want to try to get a property that doesn't actually exist. To do this, enter a restriction on the second parameter of the type.

For example:

```
function getProperty<T, K extends keyof T>(obj: T,
key: K) {
 return obj[key];
} let x = { a: 1, b: 2, c: 3, d: 4 };

 console.log(getProperty(x, "a")); // okay
//console.log(getProperty(x, "m")); // error: Argument
of type 'm' isn't assignable to 'a' | 'b' | 'c' | 'd'.
```

Using Class Types in Generalizations

When creating object factories in TS using generalizations, you must refer to class types in constructor functions. For example:

```
function
create <T>(C:
{  new():  T;
}):  T  {
                    return new c();
          }
          Class SomeClass {}
          var obj = create(SomeClass);
          console. log(obj.constructor.name);
          // shows SomeClass
```

The following example shows how to impose restrictions on the types of classes created using the class factory:

```
class
BeeKeeper
{
                    hasMask:  boolean = false;
                    }
              class Zookeper  {
                          nametag: string =
"tag";
                          }
                    class Animal  {
```

```
                    numlegs : number;
        }
        class Bee extends Animal  {
                keeper: BeeKeeper =
new BeeKeeper();

        }
        class Lion extends Animal  {
                keeper: ZooKeeper =
new ZooKeeper();

        }
        function createInstance<TAnimal
extends Animal>(c: new () => TAnimal): Tanimal
                return new c();
        }
        console.
log(createInstance(Lion).keeper.nametag); shows "tag"
        console.log(createInstance
(Bee).keeper.hasMask);  // shows "false"
```

new Keyword

To create a new object in the generalization code, we need to specify that the generalized type T has a constructor. This means that instead of the type: T parameter, we need to specify type: {new(): T;}. For example, the following generalized interface will not work:

```
function UserFactory<T>(): T {
    return new T(); // compilation error
}
```

To make the interface work, use the word *new*:

```
UserFactory<T>function (type: { new (): T;}): T {
return a new type ();
}
class
user
{

constructor () {
console.log ("User object created");
}
}
```

ENUMS

Enums allow us to define a set of named numeric constants and are defined using the enum keyword. Enumerations are subtypes of the primitive number type.

```
enum Direction {
    Up = 1,
    Down,
    Left,
    Right
}
```

The enumeration body consists of zero or more elements. The enumeration elements have a numeric value associated with the name, and can be either a constant or can be evaluated. An enumeration element is considered a constant if:

- if the value is not explicitly defined and the value of the previous member is constant. In this case, the value will be equal to the numeric value of the previous term plus 1. The exception is only the first element. If the value is not specified, it becomes 0;

- if the enumeration element is defined using a constant expression. Such expressions are a type of TS expression that can be evaluated at compile time.

An enumeration expression is constant if a numeric literal is:

- a reference to a previously defined constant element of an enumeration (it can be defined in various enumerations). If an element is defined in the same enumeration, it can be referenced using an unqualified name;

- the constant expression of the enumeration, taken in parentheses by;

- the unary operator +, -,~, applied to the constant expression of the enumeration;

- by a binary operator +, -, *, /, %, ≪, ≫, ≫, &, |, ∧ with an enumeration constant expression as an operand. A constant enumeration expression evaluated in NaN or Infinity results in a compile-time error.

In all other cases, the enumeration member is considered evaluated and its value is evaluated at the time of program execution.

```
enum FileAccess {
// constant elements
None,
Read = 1 << 1,
Write = 1 << 2,
ReadWrite = Read | Write,
// evaluated elements
G = "123".length
}
```

Enums are valid objects that exist at runtime. One reason for this is the ability to support reverse mapping from enum values to enum names.

```
enum Enum {
    A
}
let a = Enum.A;
let nameOfA = Enum[Enum.A]; // "A"
```

compiled in:

```
var Enum;
(function (Enum) {
    Enum[Enum["A"] = 0] = "A";
})(Enum || (Enum = {}));
var a = Enum.A;
var nameOfA = Enum[Enum.A]; // "A"
```

In the generated code, the enumeration is compiled into an object that stores the forward (name -> value) and reverse (value -> name) mappings. References to enum elements are always executed as property accesses and are never embedded. In many cases, this is the right solution. However, sometimes the requirements are tougher. To avoid paying the cost of additional generated code and indirect access when accessing enumeration values, you can use constant enumerations. Constant enumerations are defined using the const modifier preceding the enum keyword.

Constant Enums

In order not to generate additional code and unnecessary references to access the values of the enumerations, you can use constant enumerations.

They are defined using the const keyword, which is placed before enum. Using constant enumerations increases the performance of the code, because instead of the enumeration element, the constant associated with it is used.

```
const enum
Directions
{
                        Up,
                        Down,
                        Left,
                        Right
            }
            let directions = [Directions.Up,
Directions.Down,  Directions.Left,  Directions.Right]
```

Such enumerations should only have constant expressions, and during compilation, references to the properties of the enumeration object are replaced with values:

```
var Directions;
(function (Directions) {
    Directions[Directions["Up"] = 0] = "Up";
    Directions[Directions["Down"] = 1] = "Down";
    Directions[Directions["Left"] = 2] = "Left";
    Directions[Directions["Right"] = 3] = "Right";
})(Directions || (Directions = {}));

let directions = [0, 1, 2, 3]; //Only values here!!!
```

If we make this enumeration normal, that is, remove const, we get:

```
let directions = [Directions.Up, Directions.Down,
Directions.Left, Directions.Right]
```

Let's take look at another example:

```
Const enum Directions  {
        Up
        Down
        Right
        Left
}
```

```
function someFunc(op: Directions)  {
    switch (op)  ;
        case Directions.Up:
        // some action...
        break;
    case Directions.Down:
    // some action...
    break;
    //
 }
}
```

Now, let's see what the someFunc function will look like after compilation:

```
function
someFunc(op)
{
                        switch (op)  {
                            case 0:
                                break;
                            case 1:
                                break;
                    }
            }
```

As you can see, the corresponding constants were substituted instead of the enumeration elements.

Declare Enums

```
declare enum Enum  {
        A = 1,
        B,
        C = 2
}
```

Such enumerations are defined using the declare keyword. They are used to describe the form of existing enumerations.

The difference between such enumerations is that if an element in such an enumeration does not have an initializer, then it is considered evaluated. In normal enumerations, the opposite is true.

The compiler will not generate code for such enumerations. This can be useful when using third-party libraries (for example, jQuery, in which a certain object is defined (for example, $) when you need information about an object, but you don't need to generate code.

SYMBOLS

ECMAScript 2015 introduced the symbol type – a primitive data type similar to number and string.

Values of the *symbol* type are created by calling the Symbol constructor.

```
let sym1 = Symbol();

let sym2 = Symbol("key"); // Optional string key
```

The symbols are unchangeable and unique.

```
let sym2 = Symbol("key");
let sym3 = Symbol ("key");

sym2 = = = sym3; / / false, symbols are unique
```

Like strings, symbols can be used as keys for object properties.

```
let sym = Symbol();

let obj = {
    [sym]: "value"
};

console.log(obj[sym]); // "value"
```

Symbols can be used together with evaluated properties to declare object properties and class members:

```
const getClassNameSymbol = Symbol();

class C {
    [getClassNameSymbol]() {
        return "C";
    }
}
```

```
let c = new C();
let className = c[getClassNameSymbol](); // "C"
```

Predefined Characters
In addition to user-defined characters, there are predefined built-in characters. Embedded characters are needed to reflect the internal behavior of the language.
List of predefined characters:

- **Symbol.hasInstance:** A method that determines whether the constructor object recognizes the passed object as an instance of this constructor. Called by the *instanceof* operator.

- **Symbol.isConcatSpreadable:** A boolean value that indicates whether the object should be decomposed into array elements when used with Array. prototype. concat.

- **Symbol.iterator:** A method that returns the default iterator for an object. Called by the for-of construct.

- **Symbol.match:** A method for regular expressions that matches a regular expression to a string. Called by the *String.prototype.match* method.

- **Symbol.replace:** A method for regular expressions that replaces matched substrings in a string. Called by the *String.prototype.replace* method.

- **Symbol.search:** A method for regular expressions that returns the position in the string where the match with the regular expression is located. Called by the *String.prototype.search* method.

- **Symbol.species:** A property that contains a function that serves as a constructor for inherited objects.

- **Symbol.split:** A method for regular expressions that splits a string by the positions of matches with a regular expression. Called by the *String.prototype.split* method.

- **Symbol.toPrimitive:** A method that turns an object into the corresponding primitive value. Called by the abstract *ToPrimitive* operation.

- **Symbol.toStringTag:** A string value that is used to create a default string value that describes the object. Called by the built-in *Object. prototype.toString* method.

- **Symbol.unscopables:** An object whose proper property names are the names of properties whose bindings are not included in the environment created by the *with* construct for the corresponding objects.

CHAPTER 3

Modules and Namespaces

Modules are executed not in the global scope but in their own scope. This means that variables, functions, classes, etc. declared in the module are not visible outside the module, except when they are explicitly exported using one of the export forms. Also, to use a variable, function, class, interface, etc. exported from another module, you need to import them using one of the import forms.

WHAT IS NAMESPACE?

A namespace is a construct that is declared using the namespace keyword and is represented in the code by a regular JavaScript object.

```
namespace Identifier { }
```

The namespace mechanism is a solution to the problem of collisions in the global namespace, which has come down to our days from the time when the ECMAScript specification did not define such a thing as modules. In simple terms, namespaces are a combination of a regular global variable and an unnamed functional expression.

Constructs declared inside a namespace are broken down in an unnamed function expression. Constructs that are visible from the outside are written to the object that was referenced in the global variable passed as an argument. What to write to the global object, and what not,

DOI: 10.1201/9781003203728-3

is indicated to the compiler using the export keyword, which will be discussed very soon.

```
// @info: Before compilation

namespace NamespaceIdentifier {
  class PrivateClassIdentifier {}
  export class PublicClassIdentifier {}
}

// @info: After compilation

var NamespaceIdentifier;

(function (NamespaceIdentifier) {
  class PrivateClassIdentifier {}
  class PublicClassIdentifier {}

  NamespaceIdentifier.PublicClassIdentifier =
PublicClassIdentifier;
})(NamespaceIdentifier || (NamespaceIdentifier = {}));
```

It's also worth adding that namespace is a global declaration. This literally means that a namespace declared as global does not need to be exported or imported and a reference to it is available anywhere in the program.

WHAT IS MODULE?

Modules in TypeScript are defined using the export/import keywords and represent a mechanism for defining relationships between modules. This mechanism is internal exclusively for TypeScript and has nothing to do with ES2015 modules. They are otherwise identical to the ES2015 modules, except for the default module definition (export default).

```
// declaration.ts file
export type T1 = {};

export class T2 {}
export class T3 {}

export interface IT4 {}
export function f1() {}

export const v1 = 'v1';
export let v2 = 'v2';
export var v3 = 'v3';
```

```
// index.ts file
```

```
import {T2} from './declaration';
import * as declarations from './declaration';
```

In addition, you can even declare a namespace using the export keyword. This will limit its global scope and its use in other files will only be possible after explicit import.

```
// declaration.ts file
```

```
export namespace Bird {
  export class Raven {}
  export class Owl {}
}
// index.ts file
```

```
import { Bird } from './declaration';
```

```
const birdAll = [Bird.Raven, Bird.Owl];
```

It should be noted that you should export a namespace only when it is declared in the body of another namespace, but you need to get to it from the program.

```
namespace NS1 {
  export namespace NS2 {
    export class T1 {}
  }
}
```

Export

Any declaration (by a variable, function, class, type alias, or interface) can be exported by adding the export keyword.

Validation.ts
```
export interface StringValidator {
  isAcceptable(s: string): boolean;
}
```

ZipCodeValidator.ts
```
export const numberRegexp = /^[0-9]+$/;
```

```
export class ZipCodeValidator implements
StringValidator {
```

```
    isAcceptable(s: string) {
        return s.length === 5 && numberRegexp.test(s);
    }
}
```

Export Validation

Export definitions are useful when you need to rename the exported elements. Then, the above example can be rewritten as follows:

```
class ZipCodeValidator implements StringValidator {
    isAcceptable(s: string) {
        return s.length === 5 && numberRegexp.test(s);
    }
}
export { ZipCodeValidator };
export { ZipCodeValidator as mainValidator };
```

Reexport

Modules often extend other modules. At the same time, they themselves provide access to some of the functions of the source modules. Reexport does not perform a local import and does not create a local variable.

ParseIntBasedZipCodeValidator.ts
```
export class ParseIntBasedZipCodeValidator {
    isAcceptable(s: string) {
        return s.length === 5 && parseInt(s).
toString() === s;
    }
}

// Exports the original validator by renaming it
export {ZipCodeValidator as
RegExpBasedZipCodeValidator} from "./
ZipCodeValidator";
```

When using a module as a wrapper over one or more other modules, it is possible to reexport all their export statements at once using the export * from "module" construct.

AllValidators.ts
```
export * from ". / StringValidator"; / / exports the
'StringValidator' interface
export * from "./LettersOnlyValidator"; / / exports
the 'LettersOnlyValidator' class
```

```
export * from "./ZipCodeValidator"; / / exports the
'ZipCodeValidator' class
```

Import

Importing is almost as easy as exporting. To import an exported ad, use one of the import forms below:

Importing a Single Exported Item

```
import { ZipCodeValidator } from "./ZipCodeValidator";
let myValidator = new ZipCodeValidator();
```

the imported element can also be renamed

```
import { ZipCodeValidator as ZCV } from "./
ZipCodeValidator";
let myValidator = new ZCV();
```

Importing the Entire Module into a Single Variable, and Using It to Access the Exported Module Elements

```
import * as validator from "./ZipCodeValidator";
let myValidator = new validator.ZipCodeValidator();
```

Importing a Module for the Sake of "Side Effects"

Despite the fact that it is not recommended to do this, some modules set a certain global state that can be used by other modules. These modules may not have exported elements, or the user does not need these elements. To import such modules, use the command:

```
import "./my-module.js";
```

Default Export

Each module can contain a default export. The default export is high-lighted with the default keyword, and there can only be one such statement in a module. To import an export, a separate form of the import statement is used by default.

The default export can be very useful. For example, a library like Jquery can export jQuery or $ by default, which we probably also import under the name $ or jQuery.

JQuery.d.ts
```
declare let $: JQuery;
export default $;
```

App.ts
```
import $from "JQuery";
$("button.continue").html ("Next Step…" ) ;
```

Classes and function definitions can be immediately designated as exported by default. Such classes and functions can be declared without specifying names.

ZipCodeValidator.ts
```
export default class ZipCodeValidator {
    static numberRegexp = /^[0-9]+$/;
    isAcceptable(s: string) {
        return s.length === 5 && ZipCodeValidator.
numberRegexp.test(s);
    }
}
```

Test.ts
```
import validator from "./ZipCodeValidator";
let myValidator = new validator();
```

StaticZipCodeValidator.ts
```
const numberRegexp = /^[0-9]+$/;

export default function (s: string) {
    return s.length === 5 && numberRegexp.test(s);
}
```

Test.ts
```
import validate from "./StaticZipCodeValidator";

let strings = ["Hello", "98052", "101"];

// Использование функции validate
strings.forEach(s => {
  console.log(`"${s}" ${validate(s)?  " matches" : "
does not match"}`);
});
```

The default exported element can be a normal value:

OneTwoThree.ts
```
export default "123";
```
Log.ts
```
import num from "./OneTwoThree";
```

```
console.log(num); // "123"
```

export = import = require()

CommonJS and AMD have the concept of an exports object that contains all the module exports.

They also support replacing the exports object with a single user object. The default export is intended to replace this functionality. Both approaches, however, are incompatible. TypeScript supports the export = construct, which can be used to model the familiar way CommonJS and AMD work.

The export = construct defines a single object to export from the module. This can be a class, interface, namespace, function, or enumeration.

To import a module exported with export =, the TypeScript-specific construct import let = require("module") must be used.

ZipCodeValidator.ts
```
let numberRegexp = /^[0-9]+$/;
class ZipCodeValidator {
    isAcceptable(s: string) {
        return s.length === 5 && numberRegexp.test(s);
    }
}
export = ZipCodeValidator;
```

Test.ts
```
import zip = require("./ZipCodeValidator");

// A few test cases
let strings = ["Hello", "4546", " 101"];

// Validators
let validator = new postcode();

// For each line shows did it every validator
strings.forEach(s => {
    console.log(`"${ s }" - ${ validator.isAcceptable(s)?
"matches" : "does not match" }`);
});
```

Generating Code for Modules

Depending on the module target specified at compile time, the compiler will generate the appropriate code for Node.js (CommonJS), require.js (AMD), (UMD), SystemJS, or native ECMAScript 2015 (ES6) modules.

For more information about what the define, require, and register calls do in the generated code, see the documentation for each individual module.

This simple example shows how the names used during import and export are translated into the module loading code.

SimpleModule.ts
```
import m = require("mod");
export let t = m.something + 1;
```

AMD / RequireJS SimpleModule.js
```
define(["require", "exports", "./mod"], function
(require, exports, mod_1) {
    exports.t = mod_1.something + 1;
});
```

CommonJS / Node SimpleModule.js
```
var mod_1 = require("./mod");
exports.t = mod_1.something + 1;
```
UMD SimpleModule.js
```
(function (factory) {
    if (typeof module === "object" && typeof module.
exports === "object") {
        var v = factory(require, exports); if (v !==
undefined) module.exports = v;
    }
    else if (typeof define === "function" && define.
amd) {
        define(["require", "exports", "./mod"],
factory);
    }
})(function (require, exports) {
    var mod_1 = require("./mod");
    exports.t = mod_1.something + 1;
});
```
SimpleModule.js System
```
System.register(["./mod"], function(exports_1) {
    var mod_1;
    var t;
    return {
        setters:[
                function (mod_1_1) {
                    mod_1 = mod_1_1;
                }],
```

```
        execute: function() {
            exports_1("t", t = mod_1.something + 1);
        }
    }
});
```

Native ECMAScript 2015 SimpleModule.js Modules
```
import { something } from "./mod";
export var t = something + 1;
```

Below, we simplified the implementation of the validator from the previous example by reducing it to exporting a single named export from each module.

To compile successfully, you must specify the module target on the command line. For Node.js, used –module commonjs; for require.js — –module amd. For example:

```
tsc --module commonjs Test.ts
```

As a result of compilation, each module becomes separate. a js file. As with reference tags, the compiler will use the import statements to find and compile the dependent files.

Validation.ts
```
export interface StringValidator {
    isAcceptable(s: string): boolean;
}
```

LettersOnlyValidator.ts
```
import { StringValidator } from "./Validation";

const lettersRegexp = /^[A-Za-z]+$/;

export class LettersOnlyValidator implements
StringValidator {
    isAcceptable(s: string) {
        return lettersRegexp.test(s);
    }
}
```

ZipCodeValidator.ts
```
import { StringValidator } from "./Validation";

const numberRegexp = /^[0-9]+$/;
```

```
export class ZipCodeValidator implements
StringValidator {
    isAcceptable(s: string) {
        return s.length === 5 && numberRegexp.test(s);
    }
}
```

Test.ts
```
import { StringValidator } from "./Validation";
import { ZipCodeValidator } from "./ZipCodeValidator";
import { LettersOnlyValidator } from "./
LettersOnlyValidator";

// A few test cases
let strings = ["Hello", "98052", "101"];

// Validators
let validators: { [s: string]: StringValidator; } =
{};
validators["ZIP code"] = new ZipCodeValidator();
validators["Letters only"] = new
LettersOnlyValidator();

// For each row, shows whether it passed each
validator
strings.forEach(s => {
    for (let name in validators) {
        console.log(`"${ s }" - ${ validators[name].
isAcceptable(s)?  "matches" : "does not match" } ${
name }`);
    }
});
```

Optional Module Loading and Its Other Advanced Scenarios

In some cases, you may need to load the module only under certain conditions. In TypeScript, you can use the example below to apply this or another advanced module loading technique. This technique can be used to directly call module loaders without losing type safety.

The compiler determines for each module whether it is used in the generated JavaScript. If the module ID is only in the type descriptions and never in the expressions, then a call to require will not be generated for this module. This omission of unused links improves performance, and also allows you to organize the optional loading of modules.

The main idea of the example is that the import id = require("...") command gives access to the types that are disclosed by this module. As shown in the if block below, the module loader is called dynamically (using require). Thus, the optimization of skipping unused links is applied, which leads to loading the module only when it is needed. For this technique to work, it is necessary that the identifier defined using import is used only in the type description (i.e., never in a place in the code that will fall into the final JavaScript).

The typeof keyword is used to support type security. The typeof keyword, when used in a type description, creates a value type (the module type in this case).

Dynamic Loading of Modules in Node.js

```
declare function require(moduleName: string): any;

import { ZipCodeValidator as Zip } from "./
ZipCodeValidator";

if (needZipValidation) {
    let ZipCodeValidator: typeof Zip = require("./
ZipCodeValidator");
    let validator = new ZipCodeValidator();
    if (validator.isAcceptable("...")) { /* ... */ }
}
```

Example: dynamic loading of modules in require.js

```
declare function require(moduleNames: string[],
onLoad: (...args: any[]) => void): void;

import { ZipCodeValidator as Zip } from "./
ZipCodeValidator";

if (needZipValidation) {
    require(["./ZipCodeValidator"], (ZipCodeValidator:
typeof Zip) => {
        let validator = new ZipCodeValidator();
        if (validator.isAcceptable("...")) { /* ... */
}
    });
}
```

Example: Dynamic loading of modules in System.js

```
declare const System: any;
```

```
import { ZipCodeValidator as Zip } from "./
ZipCodeValidator";

if (needZipValidation) {
    System.import("./ZipCodeValidator").
then((ZipCodeValidator: typeof Zip) => {
        var x = new ZipCodeValidator();
        if (x.isAcceptable("...")) { /* ... */ }
    });
}
```

Working with Other JavaScript Libraries

To describe a library that is not written in TypeScript, you must declare the API provided by that library.

We call declarations that do not define implementations "ambient." They are usually set in .d.ts files. If you are familiar with C/C++, you can think of them as header files .h. Let's look at some examples.

EXTERNAL MODULES

In Node.js, most tasks are performed by loading one or more modules. We could define each module in its own file .d.ts in top-level export declarations, but it is much more convenient to put the definitions of all modules in one common .d.ts file. To do this, use a construct similar to external namespaces. It uses the module keyword and the quoted module name, which will be available for further import. For example:

node.d. ts (simplified excerpt)

```
declare module "url" {
    export interface Url {
        protocol?: string;
        hostname?: string;
        pathname?: string;
    }
    export function parse(urlStr: string,
parseQueryString?, slashesDenoteHost?): Url;
}
declare module "path" {
    export function normalize(p: string): string;
    export function join(...paths: any[]): string;
    export var sep: string;
}
```

Now we can specify / / / <reference> node.d.ts and load modules using import url = require ("url");.

```
/// <reference path="node.d.ts">
import * as URL from "url";
let myUrl = URL.parse("http://www.typescriptlang.
org");
</reference>
```

Abbreviated External Module Declaration Entry

If you don't want to spend time writing ads before you start using the new module, you can use a shortened declaration.

declarations.d.ts
```
declare module "hot-new-module";
```

All imported elements of such a module will have the type any.

```
import x, {y} from "hot-new-module";
x(y);
```

Module Declarations Using Wildcard Characters

Some module loaders, such as SystemJS and AMD, allow you to import content other than JavaScript. In such cases, a prefix or suffix is usually used to denote the special loading semantics. Module declarations using wildcard characters can be used to organize these types of downloads.

```
declare module "*!text" {
    const content: string;
    export default content;
}
// Некоторые делают это иначе
declare module "json!*" {
    const value: any;
    export default value;
}
```

You can now import elements that match"*! text " or " json!*".

```
import fileContent from "./xyz.txt!text";
import data from "json!http://example.com/data.json";
console.log(data, fileContent);
```

UMD MODULES

Some libraries are designed to be used with many module loaders or no loaders at all (global variables). They are called UMD or Isomorphic modules. You can connect such libraries either by importing them or as a global variable. For example:

math-lib.d.ts
```
export const isPrime(x: number): boolean;
export as namespace mathLib;
```

You can connect this library inside the module by importing it:

```
import {isPrime} from "math-lib";
isPrime(2);
mathLib.isPrime(2); // Error: unable to use the global
definition inside the module
```

You can also connect this library as a global variable, but this can only be done inside the script. (A script is a file without import and export commands).

```
mathLib.isPrime(2);
```

STRUCTURING MODULES

Export as Close to the Top Level as Possible

The less problems the module users have with using the exported elements, the better. Adding nesting levels makes the module more cumbersome, so you need to think carefully about its structure.

Exporting from a namespace module is just an example of adding an extra level of nesting. Although namespaces can be useful, they add another layer of abstraction to modules, which can lead to problems for users very soon and is usually not necessary.

Static methods of exported classes cause similar problems, since the class itself adds a level of nesting. It is acceptable to do this if you know exactly what you are doing, and the introduction of an additional level of nesting will add expressiveness and clearly reflect the purpose of the module. Otherwise, we recommend using the helper function.

If You Export Only One *Class* or One *Function*, Use Export *Default*

Similar to "export as close to the top level as possible," using the default export makes life easier for the users of your module. If the main task of the module is to place and export one specific element, then you should seriously consider using the default export. This approach makes both the import procedure itself and the use of imported elements a little easier. For example:

MyClass.ts
```
export default class SomeType {
  constructor() { ... }
}
```

MyFunc.ts
```
export default function getThing() { return "thing"; }
```

Consumer.ts
```
import t from "./MyClass";
import f from "./MyFunc";
let x = new t();
console.log(f());
```

This approach is optimal for users of the module. They can give your type the most convenient name for them (t in this case) and will be spared the unnecessary use of "through the dot" to search for your objects.

If You Are Exporting Multiple Objects, Put Them on the Top Level

MyThings.ts
```
export class SomeType { /* … */ }
export function someFunc() { /* … */ }
```

Accordingly, when importing:

Explicitly Define the Imported Names

Consumer.ts
```
import {SomeType, someFunc} from "./MyThings";
let x = new SomeType();
let y = someFunc();
```

Use the Namespace Import Template When Importing a Large Number of Items

MyLargeModule.ts
```
export class Dog { ... }
export class Cat { ... }
export class Tree { ... }
export class Flower { ... }
```

`Consumer.ts`

```
import * as myLargeModule from "./MyLargeModule.ts";
let x = new myLargeModule.Dog();
```

Do Not Use Namespaces in Modules

When programmers first start using module-based code organization, they often place exported elements in namespaces, thus creating additional nesting levels. But the modules have their own scope, and only the exported elements are visible from the outside. Therefore, namespaces are not able to bring tangible benefits when working with modules.

Namespaces are convenient for grouping logically related objects and global scope types, which is convenient for organizing code. For example, in C#, all collection types can be found in System.Collections. By organizing types in a hierarchy of namespaces, we make it easier for users to find them. Modules, on the contrary, in any case already exist as files. We find them by the path and file name, respectively, their logical organization is already present. You can create a directory /collections/generic/ that contains a list module.

Namespaces are an important tool for preventing name conflicts. For example, you can have My. Application.Customer.AddForm and My.Application.Order. AddForm – two types with the same name but different namespaces. And with modules, there will be no such problem. There is no good reason to create two objects with the same name inside a module. From the user's point of view, he can choose any name for the imported module, so random name conflicts are not possible.

Risk Indicators

The following is a list of warning signs regarding module structuring. Once again, make sure that you are not trying to create namespaces for your external modules, if any of the following statements apply to your situation:

- The file contains a single top-level declaration, export namespace Foo {...} (remove Foo and move everything up a level).

- The file contains a single instance of export class or export function (consider using export default).

- Multiple files contain an identical export namespace Foo {at the top level (don't count on all of them joining into a single namespace Foo!).

Loading Modules

Past topics have covered how to define and import modules in TypeScript. However, native browsers do not yet support working with modules. Maybe this feature will be implemented in a beautiful browser of the future, but at the moment you need to use special tools to load modules, which are called loaders. In this topic, we will look at loading modules using the SystemJS loader.

First of all, it is worth noting that loading from the server is done via AJAX, so such a TypeScript application must be hosted on a web server. That is, we will not be able to simply throw the page into a web browser, as, for example, it was in the first topics. Therefore, first of all, you need to decide on the web server. The web server can be anything. In this case, we will use the most democratic option - Node.js. To do this, we will only need to install it on your computer Node.js.

First, we will determine the folder on the hard disk where the project will be located. Let's say it will be folder C:\typescript. And first of all, we will define the server file in it. Let it be called server.js and will have the following code:

```
var http = require("http");
var fs = require ("fs");

http.createServer (function (request, response){

// getting the path after the slash
var filePath = request. url. substr(1);
/ / setting the default path
if (filePath == "") filePath ="index.html";
fs. ReadFile(file path, function (error, data){

if(error) { // if the file is not found
response.StatusCode = 404;
response.end ("Not found");
} more
{
response.end(data);
} return
;
})
}).listen (3000, function(){
```

```
console. log ("The server is running at http://
localhost:3000/");
```

This is the most primitive server that gives the user static files. The http.crea-teServer function is used to create a server, and the fs.ReadFile () function is used to read and send files. The server will start at http://localhost:3000/. For testing purposes, nothing else is needed in the pritsnip. But again instead of node.js this can be any other server technology-php, asp.net, python, etc.

Let's define the app directory in the project, where the TypeScript files will actually be located. Add the file devices.ts to this directory, which will represent the simplest module:

```
export interface Device{
    name: string;
}

export class Phone implements Device {
    name: string;
    constructor(n:string){
        this.name = n;
    }
}

export function Call(phone: Phone) : void{
    console.log("Make a call by", phone.name);
}
```

And also in the *app* folder, add the main application file - *app.ts* with the following code:

```
import {Phone, Call as makeCall} from "./devices";
let iphone: Phone = new Phone("iPhone X");
makeCall(iphone);
```

This file loads the devices module and uses the types defined in this module.

Now, in the root folder of the project, we will define the web page of our application-the file index.html:

```
<html>
<head>
    <meta charset="utf-8" />
    <title>TypeScript Modules</title>
</head>
```

```
<body>
    <h1>TypeScript Modules</h1>
    <div id="content"></div>

    <script src="https://cdnjs.cloudflare.com/ajax/
libs/systemjs/0.21.0/system.js"></script>
    <script>
        SystemJS.config({
            baseURL: "app",
            packages: {
                "/": { defaultExtension: "js" }
            }
        });
        System.import("app.js");
    </script>
</body>
</html>
```

First of all, SystemJS is loaded from the CDN at the bottom of the page. Next, the bootloader is configured using the SystemJS.config () function, so that it uses our files. First of all, using the baseUrl: "app" parameter, that files will be located in the app folder (where we currently have typescript files).

Since in the end we will compile TypeScript files in JavaScript (since only JavaScript is supported by the browser), then in this case we will only work with js files. To do this, we define the packages: {"/": {defaultExtension: "js"}} parameter. "defaultExtension" indicates the extension that will be added to the modules.

After that, the main application file is imported - in our case app.js (to which app.ts is compiled): System. import("app.js").

Module Resolution

Module resolution is the process used by the compiler to find out what the import command refers to. Consider the following statement: import {a} from "ModuleA." To check the correctness of the use of a, the compiler must know exactly what this element is, for which it is necessary to check the corresponding definition-ModuleA.

Relative and Nonrelative Module Imports

Module import is allowed in different ways, depending on whether the reference is relative or nonrelative.

Relative imports start with /,. /, or../. For example:

```
import Entry from "./components/Entry";
import { DefaultHeaders } from "../constants/http";
import "/mod";
```

Any other import is considered nonrelative. For example:

```
import * as $ from "jQuery";
import { Component } from "angular2/core";
```

Relative imports are allowed relative to the imported file and cannot be resolved by declaring an external module. Relative imports are best used for your modules, which are guaranteed to be in the specified location during program execution.

Nonrelative imports can be resolved relative to baseUrl or by using path mapping, which will be described below. It can also be resolved by external module declarations. Use nonrelative paths when importing any external dependencies.

Module Resolution Strategies
When the TypeScript compiler sees a nonrelative import path in the statement, it must find the file to import in the program, since the import path does not provide the necessary information about where the file is located on disk.

The TypeScript compiler uses one of the two strategies available to it to find this file. These strategies are Classic and Node. Node is the default strategy used by the TypeScript compiler, and most people prefer it because most third-party modules are Node modules.

The *classicstrategy* is present in typescript only for backward compatibility with older versions. This strategy only works if the TypeScript compiler detects nonrelative imports.

This Node strategy comes from the standard module resolution strategy in Node.js. This applies to both relative and nonrelative imports.

Classic   This strategy was previously adopted in TypeScripts by default. But now it is saved only for backward compatibility.

Relative import will be allowed relative to the imported file. So *import {b} from ". /ModuleB"* in the source file */root/src/folder/A. ts* will search for the following files:

```
/root/src/folder/moduleB.ts
/root/src/folder/moduleB.d.ts
```

For nonrelative module imports, the compiler will search the directory tree for a suitable definition file, starting with the directory containing the importing file.

For example:

Nonrelative import from *ModuleB*, such as import *{b} from "ModuleB"*, located in the source code file */root/src/folder/A.ts*, will search for *"ModuleB"* in the following locations:

```
/root/src/folder/moduleB.ts
/root/src/folder/moduleB.d.ts
/root/src/moduleB.ts
/root/src/moduleB.d.ts
/root/moduleB.ts
/root/moduleB.d.ts
/moduleB.ts
/moduleB.d.ts
```

Node   This strategy copies the behavior of a dynamic module resolution engine Node.js. See the full description of the Node resolution algorithm. js in the module documentation Node.js.

How Does Node.js Resolve Modules?
To understand which way the TS compiler will go, it is important to understand a little about the modules Node.js. Import to Node.js is executed by calling the require function. Node.js will act differently depending on whether a relative or nonrelative path is specified in require.

Using relative paths is usually not difficult. For an example, let's look at the/root/src/ModuleA file.js, which has the following import statement var x = require (". /ModuleB"); Node.js allows this import in this order:

1. As a file named /root/src/ModuleB.js, if it exists.

2. As the /root/src/ModuleB directory, if it has a package file.json, which defines the "main" module. In our example, if Node.js found the /root/

src/ModuleB/package file.json containing {"main": "lib/MainModule. js"}, then it will refer to /root/src/moduleB/lib/mainModule.js.

3. If the /root/src/ModuleB directory contains a file named index.js, by default, it is assumed that it is the main module of this directory.

However, the resolution of nonrelative module names is performed in a different way. Node will search for your modules in a special directory called node_modules. It can be at the same level of the directory hierarchy as the current file, or higher. Node will go up the directory chain, looking through each node_modules until it finds the module you tried to load.

Continuing with our example, let's assume that in /root/src/ModuleA. js used a nonrelative path, and the import command looked like this: var x = require ("ModuleB");. Node will try to resolve ModuleB to one of the following paths and will stop at the first suitable one.

```
/root/src/node_modules/moduleB.js
/root/src/node_modules/moduleB/package.json (if it
defines the "main" property)
/root/src/node_modules/moduleB/index.js

/root/node_modules/moduleB.js
/root/node_modules/moduleB/package.json (if it defines
the "main" property)
/root/node_modules/moduleB/index.js

/node_modules/moduleB.js
/node_modules/moduleB/package.json (if it defines the
"main" property)
/node_modules/moduleB/index.js
```

Additional Flags of the Module Resolution System
The initial structure of the project does not always correspond to what is obtained in the output. Usually, several steps are needed to achieve the result. This is the compilation of files .ts in .js, and copying dependencies from different sources to a single output file. As a result, the modules in the execution process can have names different from the names of the source files with their definitions. The module paths in the final output may also differ from the corresponding initial paths at the compilation stage.

TypeScript has a set of additional flags that can be used to inform the compiler about the transformations that must occur with the source code in order to generate the final output.

It is important to note that the compiler will not perform these transformations. It only uses the information it receives to perform the process of allowing the module to be imported into its definition file.

Base URL

The *baseUrl* is often used in applications that use the AMD module loader, where modules are dynamically "deployed" in a single directory. The source files of these modules can be located in different places, but the build script will put them all in the same directory.

Setting *baseUrl* tells the compiler where to look for modules. All module import commands with nonrelative names are considered relative *baseUrl*. The *baseUrl* value is defined as one of:

- the value of the baseUrl command-line argument (if a relative path is passed, it is evaluated relative to the current directory);

- the value of the baseUrl property in 'tsconfig. json' (if a relative path is passed, it is evaluated based on the location of 'tsconfig.json').

Note that setting baseUrl does not affect the relative module import commands, as they are always resolved relative to the importing files.

Path Mapping

Sometimes the modules are not directly under the baseUrl. For example, the "jquery" module import command at runtime will be converted to "node_modules\jquery\dist\jquery.slim.min.js". Loaders use the path mapping configuration to dynamically match module names and corresponding files, see the RequireJS and SystemJS documentation.

The TypeScript compiler supports declaring such mappings in the "paths" property of the tsconfig.json file. Here is an example of how you can specify the "paths" property for jquery.

```
{
    "compilerOptions": {
        "paths": {
            "jquery": ["node_modules/jquery/dist/
jquery.d.ts"]
        }
    }
}
```

The "paths" property allows you to use more complex mapping methods, including multiple backup paths. Let's look at a configuration in which only some modules are available in one location, while the rest are located in another. When you build, all these modules will be placed in one place. The project diagram may look like this:

```
projectRoot
├── folder1
|    ├── file1.ts (импортирует 'folder1/file2' и
'folder2/file3')
|    └── file2.ts
├── generated
|    ├── folder1
|    └── folder2
|         └── file3.ts
└── tsconfig.json
```

The corresponding *tsconfig.the json* will look like this:

```
{
    "compilerOptions": {
        "baseUrl": ".",
        "paths": {
            "*": [
                "*",
                "generated/*"
            ]
        }
    }
}
```

So we tell the compiler that for each module whose import statement matches the " *" pattern (i.e. any values), it must search in two places:

"*": meaning the same name without changes, so match *<moduleName>* => *<baseUrl>\<moduleName>*

"generated*" meaning the module name with the added prefix "generated," so match *<moduleName>* => *<baseUrl>\generated\<moduleName>*

Following this logic, the compiler will try to resolve the specified import instructions as follows:

import *'folder1/file2'*

- there is a match to the '*' pattern, which covers the entire module name;

- try the first replacement in the list: '*' -> *folder1/file2*;

- the result of the replacement is a relative name, we connect it *with baseUrl -> projectRoot/folder1/file2. ts*;

- The file exists. Done.

- import '*folder2/file3*'

- there is a match to the '*' pattern, which covers the entire module name;

- try the first replacement in the list: '*' -> *folder2/file3* the

- result of the replacement is a relative name, connect it to baseUrl -> *projectRoot/folder2/file3. ts.*

- The file does not exist, go to the next replacement

- the second replacement is 'generated/*' -> *generated/folder2/file3* the

- result of the replacement is a relative name, we connect it with *baseUrl -> projectRoot/generated/folder2/file3. ts.*

- The file is done.

Virtual Directories with rootDirs

Project source files located in different directories are sometimes combined at compile time to generate a single output directory. This can be thought of as creating a single "virtual" directory from a set of source directories.

Using "rootDirs," you can tell the compiler about the roots that make up this "virtual" directory, allowing the compiler to allow relative module import commands within these "virtual" directories, as if they were combined into a single directory.

For an example, let's look at the following project structure:

```
src
└── views
     └── view1.ts (imports './template1')
     └── view2.ts
```

```
generated
└── templates
        └── views
└── template1.ts (imports './view2')
```

src / views contain files with custom code for UI elements. The files in generated / templates contain the UI template binding code that is automatically generated by the template generator as part of the build. In one of the build steps, the files from /src/views and /generated/templates/views will be copied to the same directories in the output structure of the project. The view at runtime expects its template to be nearby, and it can be imported using the relative path "./template".

To indicate this relationship to the compiler, use "rootDirs." "rootDirs" defines a list of root directories (roots) whose contents need to be merged dynamically. Continuing our example, the *tsconfig file.the json* should look like this:

```
{
    "compilerOptions": {
        "rootDirs": [
            "src/views",
            "generated/templates/views"
        ]
    }
}
```

Each time the compiler encounters a relative module import in a subdirectory of one of the *rootDirs*, it tries to find that import in the *rootDirs* entries.

Tracking Module Resolution

As mentioned earlier, the compiler has the ability to go beyond the current directory when resolving modules. This behavior can make it difficult to diagnose the reasons why the module was not resolved or was resolved incorrectly. To get an idea of how the module resolution process goes, you can use the –traceResolution compiler key.

Suppose we have a simple application that uses a typescript module. App. ts contains the import instruction import * as ts from "typescript."

```
|    tsconfig.json
├───node_modules
|    └───typescript
|        └───lib
|                typescript.d.ts
└───src
        app.ts
```

Calling the compiler with the *–traceResolution* option

```
tsc -traceResolution
```

Results:

```
======== Resolving module 'typescript' from 'src/app.
ts'. ========
Module resolution kind is not specified, using
'NodeJs'.
Loading module 'typescript' from 'node_modules'
folder.
File 'src/node_modules/typescript.ts' does not
exist.
File 'src/node_modules/typescript.tsx' does not
exist.
File 'src/node_modules/typescript.d.ts' does not
exist.
File 'src/node_modules/typescript/package.json' does
not exist.
File 'node_modules/typescript.ts' does not exist.
File 'node_modules/typescript.tsx' does not exist.
File 'node_modules/typescript.d.ts' does not exist.
Found 'package.json' at 'node_modules/typescript/
package.json'.
'package.json' has 'typings' field './lib/
typescript.d.ts' that references 'node_modules/
typescript/lib/typescript.d.ts'.
File 'node_modules/typescript/lib/typescript.d.ts'
exist - use it as a module resolution result.
======== Module name 'typescript' was successfully
resolved to 'node_modules/typescript/lib/
typescript.d.ts'. ========
```

What to Look for in the Trace?

Name and location of the import statement

```
======== Resolving module 'typescript' from 'src/
app.ts'. ========
```

The strategy that the compiler follows

```
Module resolution kind is not specified,
using 'NodeJs'.
```

Loading type declarations (typings) from npm packages

```
'package.json' has 'typings' field './lib/
typescript.d.ts' that references 'node_modules/
typescript/lib/typescript.d.ts'.
```

Final result

```
======== Module name 'typescript' was successfully
resolved to 'node_modules/typescript/lib/
typescript.d.ts'. ========
```

CHAPTER 4

TS Runtime

WHAT IS RUNTIME?

Runtime is a computing environment that is necessary for the execution of a computer program and is available during the execution of a computer program. In the runtime environment, it is usually impossible to change the source code of the program, but there may be access to the operating system environment variables, object tables, and shared library modules.

Interaction with the runtime environment for interpreted programming languages is implemented directly in the interpreter, which provides interaction of language constructs with the environment in which it is run. For compiled languages, interaction with the computing environment can be implemented by a set of plug-in shared runtime libraries, or entirely in a virtual machine that executes the intermediate code into which the program is compiled.

NODE.JS

Node is a runtime environment that allows you to write server-side JavaScript (JS) code. It became very widely distributed after its release in 2011. With the growth of the code base, writing server-side JS code can be difficult due to the nature of the JS language: dynamic and weakly typed.

Node.js is not a separate programming language but a platform for using JS on the server side. If we talk about the language, then both the frontend and the backend use the same JS. The only difference is in the set of APIs that frontenders and backenders use.

DOI: 10.1201/9781003203728-4

Browser-based JS uses Web APIs that provide access to the DOM and user interface of pages and web applications. Server-side JS uses APIs that provide access to the application file system, http requests, and streams.

That is, Node.js is a technology for using JS on the backend. The features and prospects of the development of the JS language can be found in the corresponding article, and here we are talking about one of the technologies of this language.

Both are browser-based JS and Node.js runs in the V8 runtime. This engine uses your JS code, and converts it to faster machine code. Machine code is low – level code that a computer can run without having to interpret it first.

Using Node.js implements the "JavaScript for everything" paradigm. It involves using a single programming language to develop web applications instead of using different languages to work on the frontend and backend.

Most often, this platform is used to create web services that require intensive information exchange with users, including the implementation of chats, collaboration systems, social networks, etc. Many programs created on Node.js, consists of server and client parts.

WHY TYPESCRIPT IS HERE TOO?

Developers switching to JS from other languages often complain about the lack of powerful static typing, but TypeScript (TS) allows you to eliminate this drawback.

Technically speaking, TS is a superset of JS, and that means that all JS code is correct TS code.

Why Node.js?

The most significant advantage is the non-blocking I/O model. This system is event-driven and works asynchronously, lining up the queue by priority. When thousands of people connect to the server at the same time, it is easier for it to cope with the load, since there is no need to create a separate thread for each connection. Proper allocation of resources helps to withstand a larger number of connections.

WHAT IS DENO?

If you are familiar with Node.js, a popular server-side JS ecosystem, Deno is pretty much the same. Almost, but not quite.

Deno is a secure JS/TS runtime built on V8, Rust, and Tokio, providing default security and developer-friendly. The Deno runtime environment by Ryan Dahl (creator of Node.js) started developing to replace Node.js, released back in 2009, due to the lack of important, in his opinion, short-comings. Ryan's reason for thinking about Deno was due to several problems in Node.js:

- modular system and its distribution,

- support for legacy APIs,

- security issues.

Main Features of Deno

Safety

By default, Deno prohibits sensitive actions such as reading environment variables or writing to the file system.

The Deno process runs in unprivileged mode, and to access data like environment variables, you need to pass special flags.

Write permission to the file system, as well as permissions related to the environment and network, are disabled. To allow these actions, call Deno with the –allow-write and –allow-net arguments.

All interaction between the privileged Deno process and v8 is reduced to messaging (previously written in Go, now ported to Rust). This allows you to create a single point for checking all messages.

Module System

Forget about package.json and node_modules. When importing source files, you can specify either a relative or absolute path, or their full URL:

```
import { test } from "https://unpkg.com/deno_
testing@0.0.5/testing.ts"
import { log } from "./util.ts"
```

By default, all source files are cached. You can use the –reload argument to update dependencies. It works like the F5 key in the browser.

TS support out of the box

TS is supported in Deno by default. That's it. Without any "but." Without configurations.

Installation of Deno

Let's get down to business, and start with the installation, we will analyze what, where, how, and why it is installed.

Using Shell (Mac, Linux):

```
curl -fsSL https://deno.land/x/install/install.
sh | sh
```

PowerShell (Windows):

```
iwr https://deno.land/x/install/install.ps1
-useb | iex
```

Homebrew (Mac):

```
brew install deno
```

Chocolatey (Windows):

```
choco install deno
```

Scoop (Windows):

```
scoop install deno
```

Here I should warn you that installing with the help of package managers carries a danger in the form of an incomplete complete removal and update mechanism. It is best to control the versions and paths where it will be installed.

Also, to upgrade to the current version, the Deno upgrade command is provided.

Well, now let's analyze the installer itself using the example of installation in Windows.

Installation in Windows

Almost everything in Deno is based on GitHub, and the installation will be made from it, and the latest release will be taken from it.

In the future, to ensure the operation of Deno as a whole, the following files and directories will be created along the path {username}\AppData\Local\deno:

- **deps:** This directory will contain all the dependencies that were ever downloaded, grouped by the download path, and also next to each file will be a separate metadata file, which specifies the response headers, from the server that was accessed during the build, and, of course, the URL itself. This is actually the repository of your dependencies, where Deno will first turn during the launch of your project. They can also be reloaded if necessary by adding the-r flag to the Deno run command. For those who are worried about lock files and cross-dependencies, this will be described in detail in the section "Deno functionality."

- **gen:** Your js-compiled TS files will be located here. This, as you probably already understand, provides a quick start of the application after the first build.

  Compiled projects will be located here too. For example, at the path gen/file/C/dev/my_first_project

- **deno_history.txt:** This file contains a short-term history of entering commands in Deno in console mode.

- **lib.deno.d.ts, lib.deno_runtime.d.ts:** This file contains the typings of Deno core itself. You will need to know about them when you try to play with different versions of Deno.

Internal Part

- **The TS layer:** Is treated as unprivileged, which has no access to the file system or network (since they run in V8, which is a "sandbox"). This is only possible by passing messages to the Rust backend, which is "privileged." Therefore, many Deno APIs (especially filesystem calls) are implemented on the TS side as purely creating buffers for data, sending it to the Rust backend via the Rusty V8 middleware, and waiting (synchronously and asynchronously) for the result to be sent back. The functions Deno. core. send (), Deno. core. recv() do just that.

- **Rusty V8:** Is a thin layer between the TS interface and the Rust backend, serving to interact with V8 and provide only the necessary bindings. It is also used to launch V8 platforms and create/load a V8 snapshot. More information about V8 snapshots can be found on the V8 blog https://v8.dev/blog/custom-startup-snapshots. It's worth noting that the snapshot for Deno also contains a TS compiler. This allows you to significantly reduce the startup time of the compiler.

- **Rust backend:** Currently, the server side, or "privileged side," which has access to the file system, network, and environment, is implemented in Rust. For those unfamiliar with the language, Rust is a system programming language developed by Mozilla, with a focus on memory security and concurrency. It is used in projects such as Servo. The Rust backend is ported from Go, which served to create the original Deno prototype, introduced in June 2018. The reasons for the transition are related to concerns about double GC.

- **V8 is Google's JS/WebAssembly engine:** Written in C++, it is also used in particular in Google Chrome and Node.js. V8 does not support TS. Instead, all the TS code you run in Deno is compiled into JS using the TS snapshot compiler, and the generated files are stored in the. deno folder. If the user does not update the code, only cached JS files will run after the initial compilation.

- **Tokio** is an asynchronous runtime environment for Rust. It is used to create and process events. This allows Deno to spawn tasks in the internal thread pool and receive notifications to process output after the task completes. Tokio relies on Rust Future, a construct similar to Promise in JS.

Safety

Deno is safe by default. For comparison, Node.js has full access to your file system and network.

To run the program without permissions, just run the command:

```
deno run main.ts
```

If your code requires permission, you will get the following error:

```
error: Uncaught PermissionDenied: ...
```

Deno uses command-line options to explicitly allow access to various parts of the system. The most commonly used ones are

- environment
- network
- file system
- running child processes

It is recommended to allow only what is really necessary. For example, to allow reading only from a certain directory, you can use the-allow-read flag, and to enable the network to go to certain URLs, the-allow-net flag:

```
deno run -allow-read=/path -allow-net=localhost:4545
file.ts
```

If you get tired of typing all the flags each time, you can write it in the bash script or use the-A (– allow-all) flag, which I highly recommend. Or you will like Drake-an analog of make only for Deno.

Also, you can install the Deno program by using Deno install with the necessary permissions. After installation, your program will be available globally, as it will be in $PATH.

Strict: True by Default
At some point, the developers decided that this approach would ensure the reliability of the code. But, nevertheless, it is possible to remove it with a custom config.

tsconfig.json

Deno has a preset config by default, but you can set your own custom config, as in normal applications, with the exception of some options. I prefer to use decorators in TS, so there is no way without a custom config. Here is an example of running with a custom config:

```
deno run -c tsconfig.json main.ts
```

Deno Modules
One of the main major differences between Deno and Node.js is that Deno uses the official ECMAScript module standard, not the deprecated CommonJS. In Node.js ES modules only appeared at the end of 2019, with version 13.2.0, but even then, support remained immature, and it is still enabled by the controversial extension. mjs. Deno breaks out of the past, using modern web standards for its modular system.

```
import * as framework from "https://deno.land/x/
alosaur/src/mod.ts"; import {assert} from "https://
deno.land/std/testing/mod.ts";
```

As you probably noticed, unlike your usual TS code, you need to specify the file extension in the paths. This has a positive effect on the build speed of your applications. As Ryan Dahl has already noticed, not using extensions when required was an N1 design error. Node.js.

The modules can also be divided into three categories: Core, Std, X.

Deno.core

Here is the code that is necessary to ensure the work with the Rust backend.

Deno Standard Modules

https://deno.land/std/is a set of standard modules supplied by Deno developers, which guarantees their implementation together with Deno. It focuses only on the general functionality, which is enough to write any program. The standard library of the Go language was taken as a basis. Therefore, it is quite self-sufficient, due to the fact that even the testing functionality is included in the standard lib.

Deno X

This category includes everything. What was not developed by the main Deno team, as well as any import of third-party code into your application.

https://deno.land/x – is only a link shortener. And you can add your lib to this registry by sending a pull request.

JSPM, Pika.dev – sites designed primarily for converting any npm package to an ES module. For example so:

```
import HandlebarsJS from 'https://dev.jspm.io/
handlebars@4.7.6';
```

Package Manager

There has been a radical rethink regarding how package management works in Deno. Instead of relying on a central repository, it is decentralized. Anyone can place a package anywhere. There are advantages and disadvantages to using a centralized repository like npm, and this aspect of Deno is sure to be the most controversial.

No more package.json, now it is accepted to use deps.ts, in which you can describe the necessary imports as follows:

```
export {assert} from "https://deno.land/std@v0.42.0/
testing/asserts.ts";
```

You can also use the-importmap (-unstable) flag, which will allow you to describe all imports in a single json file:

```
{
  "imports": {
    "moment": "./moment/moment.ts",
    "moment/": "./moment/",
    "lodash": "./lodash/lodash.ts",
    "lodash/": "./lodash/",
    "https://www.unpkg.com/vue/dist/vue.runtime.esm.js": "./vue.ts"
  },
    "scopes": {
      "scope/": {
        "moment": "./scoped_moment.ts"
        }
      }
    }
}
```

It does not support std modules, but, nevertheless, it can work with the following schemes: file:, http:, https:.

Lock File
Deno can store and verify the integrity of subresources of modules using a small JSON file. Using the – lock = lock flag.json to enable and specify file validation. To update or create a file, use – lock = lock.json – lock-write.

Web Standards
Everything that works in Deno works the same way as in the browser by default, and Deno from the very beginning tries to ensure that there are no strange errors for Deno users. What I mean by that:

```
> reverse=a=>a.sort(n=>1)
                > reverse([1,2,3])
                                - node
(10.13.0): [3,2,1]
            - deno (0.4.0) [1,2,3]
                            - chrome (74.0)
[1,2,3]
                        - other browsers:
[1,2,3]
```

WASM, RUST, Plugins

It is worth mentioning that Deno is able to work with WASM files by default. For example, some database drivers have now been integrated in this way.

Separately, I want to say about native plugins. Since the Deno plugins are not the primary task, it cannot be downloaded directly, for example, using the usual import, and this would be strange, because in the browser you do not have this option, but nevertheless there is Deno.openPlugin. This is an asynchronous function that automatically loads the appropriate binary file, according to the platform, and caches it in the directory. deno_plugins of the current working directory.

For example:

```
const pluginOptions: PerpareOptions = {
 name: "test_plugin",
 // Whether to output log. Optional, default is true
 // printLog: true,

 // Whether to use locally cached files. Optional,
default is true
 // checkCache: true,
 // Support "http://", "https://", "file://"
urls: {
    mac: '${releaseUrl}/libtest_plugin.dylib',
    win: '${releaseUrl}/test_plugin.dll',
    linux: '${releaseUrl}/libtest_plugin.so',
 },
};
const rid = await prepare(pluginOptions);
//@ts-ignore
const { testSync } = Deno.core.ops();
const response = Deno.core.dispatch(
    testSync,
  new Uint8Array([116, 101, 115, 116])
)!;
console.log(response);
```

Debugging

Deno has built-in debugging, but at the time of this writing, the Visual Studio Code extension does not support it. To debug manually, you need to do the following:

```
deno run -A -- inspect-brk fileToDebug.ts
```

Open in Chrome *chrome://inspect*, see Target Deno, and click Inspect. This will give you debugging in the browser.

Deno has a built-in file monitoring mechanism using the Rust notification library via the Deno.watchFs () API. Deno likes to leave the hard work behind the scenes with its APIs and allows the user to implement their code as they like. If you need the – *watch* flag, then the implementation of this code is left to you.

At the moment, the most popular development tool is Visual Studio Code with the justjavac extension.vscode-deno.

Testing

The test tool is built into the Deno kernel using the Deno.test () function. Validation functions such as assert, assertEquals, etc. are included in the standard library. Therefore, the test code should look like this:

```
import { assert, assertEquals } from "https://deno.
land/std/testing/asserts.
ts";

Deno.test({
    name: "Test name",
    fn(): void {
        assert("test" === "test");
        assertEquals("test", "test");
    },
});
```

To start, you just need to type in the console:

```
deno test
```

Integration Testing

Starting the development of your framework on Deno (https://github. com/alosaur/alosaur), and by increasing the functionality on it, the need for integration tests has increased dramatically. Fortunately, Deno already had the best practices of such tests. To do this, use the function to start child processes – Deno. run(). There is a special feature of such tests: you need to release resources after passing them.

Compiler API

Deno supports runtime access to the built-in TS compiler. There are three methods in the Deno namespace that provide this access: Deno.compile () Deno.bundle () Deno.transpileOnly()

compile () – this is if you called tsc via Node.js,

bundle () is the same as compile, except that instead of returning files, it returns a single string, which is an ES module that includes all the code that was included at the time of compilation. This command is also available from the Deno bundle CLI.

For example, if the main module looked something like this:

```
export {foo} from "./foo.js";
export const bar = "bar";
```

It can be imported:

```
import {foo, bar} from "./lib.bundle.js";
```

The Bundle can also be downloaded in a web browser. Bundle is a standalone ES module, so the type attribute must be set as "module." For example:

```
<script type="module">
    import * as website from "website.bundle.js";
</script>
```

transpileOnly () is the same as transpileModule in TS. All it does is "erase" any types from the modules and generate JS. No type checking and dependency resolution.

dev_server

It was with the help of transpileOnly that dev_server was implemented – a utility for running your frontend code on Deno.

How Does It Work?

When accessing the index.html, requested by main.ts.

It is also transpiled (in accordance with the specified tsconfig), and outputs the ready-made js code at this URL.

What about Dependencies?

And here, of course, comes to the aid of jspm, cdn. pika, unpkg. Therefore, you will have to specify the appropriate importmap.

As a result, you have a JIT output, as it was in the days of systemjs.

On the plus side: you don't have to wait for the dev build to happen in the console.

But here, of course, various preprocessors are not taken into account, which now most of us do not even think about using the Angular CLI.

How ty Try It?

```
deno run -- allow-net -- allow-read -- allow-write
- unstable
```

CI and CD

Of course, for effective development, it would be impossible to do without well-built application delivery. For example, Deno itself was transferred to GitHub actions.

INSTALLING AND COMPILING THE TS

To start working with TS, install the necessary tools. There are two ways to install TS: via the npm package manager or as a plugin for Visual Studio.

Installation via NPM

To install via npm, you must first install Node.js (if it was not previously installed). After installing Node.js you need to run the following command in a command prompt (Windows) or terminal (Linux):

```
npm install -g typescript
```

When installing on macOS, you also need to enter the sudo command. When you enter this command, the terminal will ask for the user's username and password to install the package:

```
sudo npm install -g typescript
```

It is possible that TS was already installed earlier. In this case, you can update it to the latest version using the command:

```
npm update -g typescript
```

To check the version, enter the command:

```
tsc -v
```

Installing as a Visual Studio Plugin

If we use Visual Studio, then when it is installed, all the necessary tools for working with TS are automatically installed, and we do not need to take any additional actions.

So, after installing the development tools for TS on the path C:\Program Files (x86)\Microsoft SDKs\TypeScript\[version_number] we can see all the installed files, including the compiler file itself tsc.exe.

Compiling an App

First, create the application directory. In my case, it will be a folder along the path C:/typescript. Add the file to the directory index.html. Open this file in any text editor and define the following code[1] in it:

```
<!DOCTYPE html>
<html>
<head>
    <meta charset="utf-8" />
    <title>TypeScript HTML App</title>
</head>
<body>
    <h1>TypeScript HTML App</h1>
    <div id="content"></div>
    <script src="app.js"></script>
</body>
</html>
```

This is a normal html file where the file is attached app.js. Now, in the same directory, create the app.ts file. And it is app.ts, not app.js, that is, the TS code file. It is also a plain text file. And in it we define the following content:

```
ar el = this.document.getElementById("content");

class user{
```

---

[1] The codes in this chapter are derived from https://www.npmjs.com/package/typescript.

```
name : string;
age : number;
constructor (_name:string, _age: number) {

this.name = _name;
this. age = _age;
}
}

var tom : User = new user ("Jack", 29);
el. innerHTML = "Name:" + jack.name + " age:" + jCK.
age;
```

Here, we get the element with id=content, and create the User class. Next, we'll look at creating and using classes. Creating an object of this class with the name Jack and the age of 29 years. And output the object data to the element. When saving a file, it is better to choose utf-8 encoding.

Now let's compile this file. To do this, in the command line/terminal, use the cd command to go to the directory where the app.ts file is located (in my case, this is C:\typescript). And to compile, run the following command:

```
tsc app.ts
```

After compilation, an app file is created in the project directory.js, which will look like this:

```
var el = this.document.getElementById("content");
var User = (function () {
    function User(_name, _age) {
        this.name = _name;
        this.age = _age;
    }
    return User;
}());
var jack = new User("Jack", 29);
el.innerHTML = "Name: " + jack.name + " age: " + jack.
age
```

MERGING DECLARATIONS

TS uses several unique principles to describe JS objects at the type level. One example of such a completely exclusive principle for TS is "ad merge." Understanding how this mechanism works gives you an advantage when working with existing JS code, and also opens the door to more complex abstraction principles.

In this chapter, "merging declarations" means that the compiler combines two separate declarations with the same name into a single definition. The resulting definition has properties that are common to both source declarations. Not only two ads can be combined, but any number of ads can be combined.

Basic Concepts

In TS, a declaration creates entities in at least one of three groups: namespaces, types, or values. Namespace-creating declarations create namespaces that contain names that are accessible through the dot syntax. The type-creating declarations create a type with the described form that is bound to the specified name. Finally, value-generating declarations create values that are available in the generated JS code.

Declaration Type	Namespace	Type	Value
Namespace	X		X
Class		X	X
Enumeration		X	X
Interface		X	
Type Alias		X	
Function			X
Variable			X

Understanding what is created by a particular ad helps you understand how the merge occurs.

Merging Interfaces

The simplest and perhaps most commonly used type of merge is interface merge. At the simplest level, such a merge mechanically merges the members of both declarations into a single interface with the same name.

```
interface Box {
    height: number;
    width: number;
```

```
}

interface Box {
    scale: number;
}

let box: Box = {height: 5, width: 6, scale: 10};
```

Interface members that are not functions must be unique. The compiler will throw an error if both interfaces define a member with the same name that is not a function.

Each member function with the same name is treated as an overload description for the same function. It is also worth noting that when merging interface A with a subsequent interface A, the second one will have a higher priority than the first one.

So, in this example:

```
interface Cloner {
    clone(animal: Animal): Animal;
}

interface Cloner {
    clone(animal: Sheep): Sheep;
}

interface Cloner {
    clone(animal: Dog): Dog;
    clone(animal: Cat): Cat;
}
```

Three interfaces will be merged together and you will get the following ad:

```
interface Cloner {
    clone(animal: Dog): Dog;
    clone(animal: Cat): Cat;
    clone(animal: Sheep): Sheep;
    clone(animal: Animal): Animal;
}
```

Note that the elements within the groups retain their order, but the groups themselves are ordered so that the later overloads are at the beginning.

The only exception around this rule is specialized signatures. If the signature has a parameter with the type of a single string literal (i.e., not a union of string literals, for example), then it will rise to the top of the combined list of overloads.

Merging Namespaces

Like interfaces, members of namespaces with the same names are also combined. Since declaring a namespace creates both a namespace and a value, you need to understand how they are all combined.

To merge namespaces, the type declarations from the exported interfaces in each of the namespaces are combined to form a single namespace with the combined interface definitions inside.

When merging namespace values, each definition is taken, and if a namespace with that name already exists, it is expanded by adding exported members from the second namespace.

In this example, the combined declaration is Animals:

```
namespace Animals {
    export class Zebra { }
}

namespace Animals {
    export interface Legged { numberOfLegs: number; }
    export class Dog { }
}
```

equivalent to:

```
namespace Animals {
    export interface Legged { numberOfLegs: number; }

    export class Zebra { }
    export class Dog { }
}
```

This namespace merge model is not bad to start with, but you need to understand what happens to members that are not exported. Non-exported members are only visible in the original (non-merged) namespace. This means that after the merge, they will not be visible to members from other ads. This can be seen more clearly in the following example:

```
namespace Animal {
    let haveMuscles = true;
```

```
export function animalsHaveMuscles() {
    return haveMuscles;
}
}

namespace Animal {
    export function doAnimalsHaveMuscles() {
        return haveMuscles;   // <-- error, haveMuscles
isn't seen here
    }
}
```

Since haveMuscles is not exported, it is only visible in the animalsHave-Muscles function from the same unconnected namespace. The doAnimalsHaveMuscles function, although included in the combined Animal namespace, does not see the non-exported member.

Merging Namespaces with Classes, Functions, and Enumerations

Namespaces are flexible enough to be combined with other types of declarations. To do this, the namespace declaration must be placed after the declaration to be merged with. The resulting ad will have the properties of both source ads. This feature is used in TS to model a number of techniques from JS and other programming languages.

Merging Namespaces with Classes
This allows you to describe nested classes.

```
class Album {
    label: Album.AlbumLabel;
}
namespace Album {
    export class AlbumLabel { }
}
```

The visibility rules for the merged members are the same as those described in the "Merging Namespaces" section, so AlbumClass must be exported to be visible in the merged class. The final result is a class used from inside another class. You can also use namespaces to add static members to existing classes.

In addition to the nested class technique, you are probably familiar with the practice from JS of creating a function that is then extended by adding properties to it. In order to create such structures type-safe, TS uses ad merge:

```
function buildLabel(name: string): string {
    return buildLabel.prefix + name + buildLabel.
suffix;
}

namespace buildLabel {
    export let suffix = "";
    export let prefix = "Hello, ";
}
alert(buildLabel("Sam Smith"));
```

Prohibited Merges

Not all merges are allowed. Currently, classes cannot be combined with other classes or with variables.

In addition to the traditional OO hierarchy, there is a way to create classes from reusable components by combining simpler incomplete classes. The idea of mix-ins or traits is also used in languages such as Scala. This approach has also gained some traction in the JS user community.

The following code demonstrates the use of impurity in TS. The example will be followed by a detailed explanation.

```
// Disposable mixin
class Disposable {
    isDisposed: boolean;
    dispose() {
        this.isDisposed = true;
    }

}

// Activatable mixin
class Activatable {
    isActive: boolean;
    activate() {
        this.isActive = true;
    }
    deactivate() {
        this.isActive = false;
    }
}
```

```
class SmartObject implements Disposable, Activatable {
    constructor() {
        setInterval((() => console.log(this.isActive +
" : " + this.isDisposed), 500);
    }

    interact() {
        this.activate();
    }
    // Disposable
    isDisposed: boolean = false;
    dispose: () => void;
    // Activatable
    isActive: boolean = false;
    activate: () => void;
    deactivate: () => void;
}
applyMixins(SmartObject, [Disposable, Activatable]);
let smartObj = new SmartObject();

setTimeout(() => smartObj.interact(), 1000);


//////////////////////////////////////////
// Somewhere in your dynamic library
//////////////////////////////////////////

function applyMixins(derivedCtor: any, baseCtors:
any[]) {
    baseCtors.forEach(baseCtor => {
        Object.getOwnPropertyNames(baseCtor.
prototype).forEach(name => {
            derivedCtor.prototype[name] = baseCtor.
prototype[name];
        });
    });
}
```

The code[2] begins with the definition of two classes that will be used as impurities. Each of them is aimed at demonstrating a certain activity or

---

[2] The codes in this chapter are derived from https://www.typescriptlang.org/docs/handbook/mixins.html.

opportunity. Later, we will mix them to form a new class that combines their properties.

```typescript
// Disposable mixin
class Disposable {
    isDisposed: boolean;
    dispose() {
        this.isDisposed = true;
    }

}
// Activatable mixin
class Activatable {
    isActive: boolean;
    activate() {
        this.isActive = true;
    }
    deactivate() {
        this.isActive = false;
    }
}
```

Next, we will create a new class that will combine both admixtures. Let's look at how to achieve this:

```typescript
class SmartObject implements Disposable, Activatable {
```

The first thing you might have noticed is that implements is used instead of extends. This approach allows you to treat classes as interfaces and use only the types Disposable and Activatable, and not their implementations. It turns out that we will have to create the implementation in a new class. But the problem is that this is exactly what we would like to avoid when using impurities.

To avoid doing the implementation again, we create stand-in properties, whose types will be derived from the corresponding impurities. It is sufficient for the compiler to have these elements available dynamically. This approach allows us to take advantage of the impurities, but with the additional burden of taking into account such nuances.

```
// Disposable
isDisposed: boolean = false;
dispose: () => void;
// Activatable
isActive: boolean = false;
activate: () => void;
deactivate: () => void;
```

As a result, we combine our admixtures in a class, creating a complete implementation.

```
applyMixins(SmartObject, [Disposable, Activatable]);
```

Let's write an auxiliary function designed to create impurities. It will run through the properties of the impurities and copy them to the target element, filling the duplicate properties with their implementations.

```
function applyMixins(derivedCtor: any, baseCtors:
any[]) {
    baseCtors.forEach(baseCtor => {
        Object.getOwnPropertyNames(baseCtor.
prototype).forEach(name => {
            derivedCtor.prototype[name] = baseCtor.
prototype[name];
        });
    });
}
```

CHAPTER 5

Typescript Architecture

As we know, TypeScript was created by Microsoft to facilitate the creation of large-scale JavaScript applications. Some TypeScript features, such as modules or classes, can make it easier to build large applications, but this is not enough. We need a strong application architecture if we want to be successful in the long run. In this chapter, we will look at all the aspects you need to create an application.

WHAT IS AN APPLICATION ARCHITECTURE?

An application architecture is a set of methods and patterns that help developers create structured applications. Architecture is, first of all, a global thing. Its understanding is necessary not in the context of a specific programming language. You need to understand the key ideas in general to understand how the benefits of using a particular architecture are achieved.

WHY DO WE NEED ARCHITECTURE?

The architecture is needed to save time during the development process, maintain the testability and extensibility of the system over a long period of development.

Initially, on building a good and clear architecture, as a result, we get the following advantages:

- It is cheaper to maintain the code (hence, less time and financial costs).

DOI: 10.1201/9781003203728-5

- Simplify the testability of the code (hence, you will need fewer testers and lower losses due to missed "bugs on the prod").

- Accelerate the introduction of new developers into the project.

To ensure the stable operation of complex web applications, it is desirable to use technologies that will give the best performance and speed. There are two ways to develop web applications: single-page applications (SPA) and multi-page applications (MPA).

SINGLE-PAGE APPLICATION

Single-page applications allow you to simulate the work of desktop applications. The architecture is designed in such a way that when you go to a new page, only part of the content is updated. This way, there is no need to re-load the same items. This is very convenient for developers and users. For SPA development, one of the most popular programming languages is used – JavaScript. Regardless of which structure of the future web application you choose, pay attention to the graphics and user interface.

Main advantages of SPA:

- **Performance:** Since SPA does not update the entire page but only the necessary part, this significantly increases the speed of work.

- **High speed of development:** Readymade libraries and frameworks provide powerful tools for developing web applications. Backend and frontend developers can work on the project in parallel. Thanks to a clear separation, they will not interfere with each other.

- **Mobile apps:** SPA makes it easy to develop a mobile application based on readymade code.

MULTI-PAGE ARCHITECTURE

Multi-page applications have a more classic architecture. Each page sends a request to the server and completely updates all the data, even if the data is small. Thus, performance is wasted on displaying the same elements. Accordingly, this affects the speed and performance.

Many developers use JavaScript to increase speed and reduce load. A good example is updating products without reloading the page, when using filters in an online store. This is much more convenient and, most importantly, faster. The main advantages of Multi-Page Application (MPA) are

- **Easy SEO optimization:** The MPA architecture makes it quite easy to optimize each page for search engines.

- **Easy development:** Typically, developing a multi-page application requires a smaller stack of technologies.

- **Lots of solutions.**

Each architecture has its own advantages and disadvantages and is well suited for a particular type of project. SPA is distinguished by its speed and the ability to develop a mobile application based on readymade code. But at the same time, SPA has poor SEO optimization. Thus, this architecture is an excellent approach for SaaS platforms, social networks, closed communities, where search engine optimization does not matter.

MPA is more suitable for creating large online stores, business sites, catalogs, marketplaces, etc. A well-optimized MPA has high speed and performance, but still does not allow you to easily develop a mobile application. MPA and SPA with the right architecture are well suited for developing scalable web applications.

CREATING AN APPLICATION IN TYPESCRIPT

As an example, we will write a simple function that will output messages to the console.
What a function should be able to do:

- Output a message

- Attach to the message any data that needs to be logged in

- [Optional] Add a prefix to the message to understand which module outputs the log

- [Optional] Color the message depending on the type: log (normal message), info (notification), warn (warning), error (error)

  ```
  _log(<message>, <arg>, <prefix>,
  <type>);
  ```

Something like this:

```
_log('Here is our user id:', 123);
_log('Here is our user id:', 123, 'User Profile',
'info');
```

MAKING AN APP

Let's create a new project, and in it a file, logger.ts.

As we have already found out, _log will have four parameters. Since TypeScript is a statically typed language, you need to describe the type of each argument.

message – type String

arg – data for logging, of any type. For such cases, TypeScript has the any type.

prefix – the String type.

type ᵧ the message style. You can create logs in any way, but for simplicity we will use readymade Console API methods: log, info, warn, error. To protect yourself from passing any other types, you must Strongly list the allowed values. To do this, create a custom ConsoleMethod data type.

```
type ConsoleMethod = 'log' | 'info' | 'warn' |
'error';

function _log(message: string, args: any, prefix:
string, type: ConsoleMethod = 'log'): void {

        prefix  = prefix? prefix + ': ' : '';
        message = prefix + message;

        console[type](message, args);
}

// Example of a call
_log('Test logging message', 123, 'Logger', 'info');
```

Compile .ts in .js. To do this, run the command in the project directory:

```
tsc logger.ts
```

If no errors occurred during compilation, the file should appear logger.js. At the same time, if somewhere in our application there is a log with an incorrect type, we will see a compilation error. Let's replace the example call with an erroneous one:

```
_log('Test logging message', 123, 'Logger',
'debug');
```

That is, by strongly typing the arguments, we protected ourselves from errors when calling our method. If you type all the methods of the application in this way, its stability will increase. In addition, the compiler will not allow you to build a script with syntax errors.

COMPILATION: WATCH MODE

To avoid running the compilation manually each time, you can enable automatic recompilation when files are changed:

```
tsc *.ts -watch
```

MV* ARCHITECTURE

Many tasks that would normally be performed on the server side are performed on the client side in SPAs. This has led to an increase in the size of JavaScript applications and the need for more effective code organization.

As a result, developers have started using some of the design patterns that have been successfully used in the back end over the past decade in the interface. These include the Model-View-Controller (MVC) design pattern and some of its derived versions, such as Model-View-ViewModel (MVVM) and Model-View-Presenter (MVP).

Developers around the world have started sharing some SPA frameworks that somehow try to implement the MVC design pattern, but don't necessarily Strongly follow the MVC pattern. Most of these frameworks implement Models and Views, but since not all of them implement controllers, we call this family of frameworks MV*.

MVC (MODEL VIEW CONTROLLER)

The MVC pattern (Model-View-Controller or Model-State-Behavior) describes a simple way to build an application structure that aims to separate business logic from the user interface. As a result, the application is easier to scale, test, maintain, and of course implement.

MVC is an architecture with three layers:

- **Models:** Manage the data of an application. The models will be anemic (they will lack functionalities) since they will be referred to the services.

- **Views:** A visual representation of the models.

- **Controllers:** Links between services and views.

Model

The model in MVC provides the data. As a rule, this is a very simple POJO (Plain Old JavaScript Object – good old Java object), which has certain properties. As an example of a model, consider the following TypeScript class:

```
interface IModel {
    DisplayName: string;
    Id: number;
}
class Model implements IModel {
    DisplayName: string;
    Id: number;
    constructor(model : IModel) {
    this.DisplayName = model.DisplayName;
    this.Id = model.Id;
}
}
let firstModel = new Model({Id: 1, DisplayName:
'firstModel'});
```

Here, we have defined an interface called IModel, which has the properties Id and DisplayName, and a class that implements this interface. We have provided a simple constructor to set these properties. The last line of this fragment creates an instance of this class with the desired properties. As you can see from this snippet, the Model class is a very simple POJO that contains some data.

View

The view in MVC provides a visual representation of the model. In web frameworks, this will usually be a snippet of HTML code:

```
<div id="viewTemplate">
    <span> {Id} </span>
    <span><h1> {DisplayName} </h1></span>
</div>
```

There is a div tag here that contains two span tags. The contents of the first span tag are highlighted in bold and will display the Id property from the model. The content of the second span tag is the h1 header and displays the DisplayName property from the model. By separating the elements of the user interface view from the model, we can see that we can change the view as we like, even without using the model code. We can apply styles to each element using CSS, or even completely hide certain properties in the view. This separation gives us the ability to design or modify a part of the display regardless of the model.

This design work can even be transferred to a completely separate and independent team with specialized skills in the field of user interface design. As long as the underlying model doesn't change, both parts of the model and view will work together seamlessly.

Let's look at the following example:

```
class View {
    template: string;
    constructor(_template: string) {
    this.template = _template;
    }
    render(model: Model) {
    // Combining the template and the view;
    }
}
```

Here, we have defined a View class that has a single template property. When we create this view, we give it an HTML template that it should use. This View class also has a render method with a single model argument. The render method will combine the template and the model and return the final HTML code.

Controller

The controller in the MVC framework does the job of coordinating the interaction between the model and the view. The controller usually performs the following steps:

- Creates an instance of the model

- Creates an instance of the view

- Passes an instance of the model to the view

- Asks the view to visualize itself (generate the actual HTML code based on the values in the model)

- Attaches the resulting HTML code to the DOM tree

The controller in MVC is also responsible for the application logic. This means that it can control which views are presented, when and what to do when certain events occur.

As an example of what a controller might look like, let's look at the following code:

```
class Controller {
    model: Model;
    view : View;
    constructor() {
        this.model = new Model({Id : 1, DisplayName :
'firstModel'});
        this.view = new View($('#viewTemplate')
.html());
    }
    render() {
        $('#domElement').html(this.view.render
(this.model));
    }
}
```

Here we have defined the Controller class, which has the model and view properties. Then our constructor function creates an instance of the Model class with certain properties and an instance of the View class. An instance of the View class is created using a template that is read from the viewTemplate DOM element. The Controller class also defines the render function, which sets the actual HTML code of the DOM element DOMElement. This HTML code is the result of calling the render function for the View class and passing the model for rendering.[1]

Let's see how the process itself goes:

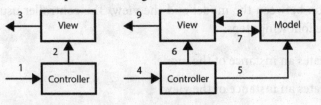

---

[1] The image is taken from https://habr.com/en/post/151219/.

1. When a user visits a web resource, the initialization script creates an instance of the application and runs it for execution.

2. The index action of the front controller is executed, which generates a view of the main page.

3. The view is displayed to the user.
   The first three steps are a simple chain, without using a model. Next is the sequence where the model is involved:

4. After the application receives a request from the user, an instance of the requested controller is created and the specified action is called.

5. This action calls the methods of the model that modify it.

6. The view is generated (or the view is notified when the model is updated).

7. The view requests data to be displayed.

8. The model returns the requested data.

9. The view displays the results to the user.

MVC FRAMEWORKS

One of the most important moments in the history of TypeScript development was when it was announced that the Microsoft and Google teams were working together on Angular 2. Angular 2 was a long-awaited update to the popular Angular framework. But unfortunately, this update required a new set of language features to make the Angular 2 syntax cleaner and clearer. Google originally proposed a new language called AtScript to simplify these new language features, which were also closely related to the ECMAScript 6 and 7 offerings.

After some time of collaboration, it was announced that all the necessary features of the AtScript language would be included in TypeScript and that Angular 2 would be written in TypeScript. This meant that the vendors of the new language features (TypeScript and Microsoft) and the consumers of the new language features (Angular 2 and Google) were able to agree on the requirements and the near future of the language. From this cooperation, it can be understood that the TypeScript language has been thoroughly studied by a well-known JavaScript development team and has come a long way. However, Angular 2 was not the first framework to adopt the TypeScript language. Many third-party JavaScript libraries also offer full TypeScript support.

Using the MVC framework provides a number of advantages like:

- Separation of the various elements used to display information to the user

- Increased flexibility and reuse

- A single model can have several different views that can be used at different times

- User interface development activities can be undertaken by a team of specialists

- Changes to the model data can trigger events in a completely different controller, and each component does not know about the other

- Views can contain other views in a nested way, thereby improving reuse

- Changes in the behavior of a component can be made without changing its visual representation (by changing the controller, not the representation)

- Fast and parallel development

- Testability of individual components

BACKBONE

We will start our research on TypeScript frameworks by creating an application in Backbone. While it can be argued that Backbone is not a TypeScript framework, we have already seen how it can be used with TypeScript syntax. Backbone is also one of the oldest frameworks. It's small, light, and extremely fast. Backbone, however, requires writing a little more code, compared to most frameworks, since it is actually the groundwork of the MVC framework.

When working with Backbone, you will need to call the visualization functions yourself, as well as manually attach the rendered HTML code to the DOM tree. To make development on Backbone a little easier, the Marionette framework was developed on top of Backbone, to simplify and remove most of the code that is being used. In fact, there are a number of frameworks that use Backbone as the main framework and add additional concepts that are useful when creating web applications. Marionette is also extremely fast, as it adds only a thin layer of functionality on top of Backbone, while still using the basic Backbone library.

Backbone.js is a JavaScript library. It uses a RESTful JSON interface. It is based on the Model-View-Presenter (MVP) application design pattern. This library is designed for developing single-page web applications. It helps to keep various parts of web applications in sync.

Setting up the environment for Backbone is quite simple and can be done via tsc and npm as follows. Initialize the TypeScript environment with tsc:

```
tsc-init
```

Initialize npm and install Backbone, Bootstrap, JBone, and the declaration files for Backbone using the @types:

```
npm syntax init
npm install backbone
npm install bootstrap
npm install jbone
npm install @types/backbone
```

JBone is a jQuery implementation built specifically for Backbone. It includes all the jQuery functionality that Backbone requires, and is significantly lighter and faster than the full jQuery library.

AURELIA

Aurelia was one of the first SPA frameworks to offer full TypeScript integration. It is a framework that uses the capabilities of ECMAScript 6 to improve the development experience. One of the most striking features of Aurelia is the small amount of code you need to write to get things done.

Aurelia understands that if you are writing a standard class, you will probably want to use the class properties to render the HTML code. Of all the frameworks that we will discuss, Aurelia is the easiest to use and the most intuitive. There are no hidden bugs or special workarounds. This framework has gone to great lengths to simplify the TypeScript development process.

The easiest way to set up a development environment is to use the Aurelia command-line interface aurelia-cli, which can be installed as follows:

```
npm install aurelia-cli -g
```

After installation, you can call it to create a new project:

```
au new
```

You will be asked a simple set of questions, starting with the name of the base catalog you would like to use. The next question is whether to use ESNext or TypeScript as the development language, and the last question is whether or not to load all the project dependencies. Select TypeScript and then Yes to load the dependencies. It will take a few minutes to set up the default project structure. After that, a new directory will be created based on the project name you selected at the beginning of the process.

The aurelia-cli program has several options. To compile your project, enter:

```
au build
```

To launch the Aurelia app, enter:

```
au run
```

This is followed by the compilation and binding steps, and then configuring the http server to serve the default application on port 9000.

ANGULAR

Angular is an open-source framework for creating frontend web applications. It is aimed at solving several problems that a developer faces when building single-page applications. This framework simplifies application development and testing. It implements the Model-View-Controller (MVC) and Model-View-View-Model (MVVM) approaches.

Since its release, its ecosystem has gone beyond imagination. Now it is deservedly called the most used JS framework for developing SPA (Single-Page-Applications), and it boasts the largest developer community.

Angular 2 comes with a large list of features that will allow you to develop everything from web to desktop and mobile applications. The framework is built on typescript from Microsoft with an eye to making JavaScript code more flexible and attractive for large enterprises.

Angular 2 is a completely rewritten Angular 1 framework that used TypeScript as the preferred language. The naming convention adopted by the Angular team states that Angular 1 is now called AngularJS, and Angular versions 2 and higher are called Angular. Since the release of Angular 2, the Angular team has released a number of major updates, and the current version of Angular at the time of writing this chapter is Angular 7. The examples in this book are written using Angular 7, so wherever you see the word Angular, remember that it refers to Angular version 7. In this section, we will look at how the Model-View-Controller design pattern is used in Angular.

Similar to configuring the development environment in Aurelia, Angular also has a tool for configuring the project using the command line called "Angular Command Line Interface." It can be installed using npm by the following way:

```
npm install -g @angular/cli
```

Once the command-line interface is installed globally, we can configure the Angular development environment using the command-line interface:

```
ng new my-app
```

The Angular command line interface is designated as ng, and here we have specified that it should create a new project in a new directory named my-app. In the new directory, the command-line interface will download and install all the necessary components of the Angular application, as well as create a minimal project instance in the src/app directory to get you started. To start the development web server and see how this application works, type the following command:

```
npm start
```

The start command will compile all the source code of the application and launch the web server on port 4200.

Along with compiling the application and automatically starting the web server, the npm start command will also look at the source files in the project directory and automatically recompile the application after changing the files. It will also give the web browser a signal to restart the app. The built-in monitoring, recompilation, and reloading capabilities are very helpful in web application development, providing quick feedback when the source code changes. Keep an eye on the console where you are running npm start. It shows all TypeScript compilation errors that occur when saving your files.

REACT

Despite the fact that React is more of a library than a framework, it stands behind the user interface of Facebook and Instagram, showing its effectiveness inside dynamic applications with high traffic (bandwidth).

It is rightfully considered the fastest growing JS framework: today there are about 1000 GitHub authors. In the MVC (Model-View-Controller) React model.js acts as a "V" and can be easily integrated into any architecture. Thanks to the use of a virtual DOM tree, it provides a greater performance boost compared to Angular 1.x. In addition, React components can be created and reused in other applications, or even transferred for public use.

Although React is more difficult to learn, it makes application development simple and easy to understand. In addition, it can be ideally suited for complex, impressive software solutions with a high degree of load.

It uses a specific built-in syntax to combine HTML templates and JavaScript code into a single file called JSX. It doesn't have downloadable string templates, like in Backbone, or HTML code snippets that are in a separate file, like in Angular or Aurelia. In React, all templates are mixed with regular JavaScript code, using an HTML-like syntax. As a simple example of this syntax, let's look at the following code:

```
render() {
    return <div>Hello <span>React</span></div>;
}
```

Here, we have the standard TypeScript render function. As part of this function, we return what looks like native HTML code with <div>tags and child <span>tags. Note that there are no quotation marks around these HTML elements. They are written inside our function without a clear separation from the regular TypeScript code.

TypeScript included support for the unique React/JSX syntax in release 1.6. However, to use the new JSX syntax, we will need to create

Typescript files with the extension .tsx instead of the usual extension. ts. When TypeScript finds files with the extension. tsx, it parses the file as a JSX file, which allows you to use the JSX syntax.

The process that React uses to generate JavaScript from JSX files is an additional step in the normal development workflow. Our TypeScript files *.tsx*, after compilation, will generate JavaScript files that convert the JSX syntax into a series of calls to React libraries.

For example, using the <*div*> element in *.tsx* file will create a call to *React.createElement* ("div",…) in the compiled JavaScript file. These compiled files must then be combined with the React libraries themselves to create executable code. For this reason, it is recommended to use a tool such as Webpack to combine the output of the compilation step with the React libraries. Webpack will also create a single output file to load into the browser in a process called bundling.

To start a new React project, we will follow a few steps. First, create a directory for your project and initialize npm:

```
mkdir react-sample
cd react-sample
npm init
```

Here, we create a directory for our project, go to it, and initialize npm in the project directory. After that, the package file will be created.json, which can use npm. After initialization, we can install webpack:

```
npm install -g webpack
npm install -g webpack-cli
```

The webpack will be installed as a global Node module and the webpack command-line interface, webpack-cli, will be installed. Note that, although we have webpack installed globally, the webpack command-line tool should still find webpack modules in the node_modules directory. This means that we also need to install webpack as a local module.

```
npm install webpack -save-dev
npm install webpack-cli -save-dev
```

Now we can install React:

```
npm install react react-dom
```

After that, the react and react-dom libraries will be installed in the node_ modules directory. We will need a number of other utilities, namely:

```
npm install -save-dev ts-loader source-map-loader
```

After that, the *ts-loader* and *source-map-loader* utilities will be installed as development dependencies. We will also need to install Boostrap as we did in our previous projects:

```
npm install bootstrap
```

After installing Bootstrap, we can install react ad files using the @types syntax:

```
npm install @types/react --save-dev
npm install @types/react-dom --save-de
```

Webpack Configuration

As indicated earlier, webpack is used to combine TypeScript output with React libraries and create a single unified JavaScript file that can be used in the browser. To do this, however, use the compilation options for TypeScript in the tsconfig file.json and webpack configuration in the webpack.config file.the js must be consistent. The easiest way to do this correctly is to use one of the convenient configuration tools available online. One of these tools can be found on the page https://webpack.jakoblind. no. It provides a simple HTML page for configuring a number of options available for webpack.

In this chapter, we took a detailed look at what an MVC framework is, and discussed each of its elements. We have covered the roles and responsibilities of the model, view, and controller in MVC, and how they interact with each other when creating user interfaces. We also briefly discussed the benefits of using MVC frameworks. We then explored four MVC frameworks that are either very tightly integrated with TypeScript or written with TypeScript in mind. We also discussed the factors that affect performance when working with each of these frameworks.

TEST-DRIVEN DEVELOPMENT

In this chapter, we will look at test-driven development in relation to TypeScript. We will discuss some of the most popular testing frameworks, write some unit tests using these frameworks, and then discuss the libraries for unit testing and methods for continuous integration.

Test-driven development is a way to reflect on our code, which should be part of the standard development process. It is a development paradigm that starts with tests and drives the driving force of production code through these tests. Test-driven development is like asking a question: How do I know I've solved a problem? This is an important idea to understand. We are writing code to solve the problem, but we must be able to prove that we have solved the problem with the help of automated tests.

The main stages of this approach are

- Writing a test that doesn't pass

- Running a test to make sure it doesn't pass

- Writing code to pass the test

- Running a test to make sure it passes

- Running all the tests to see that the new code doesn't break the other one

- Repetition

Using test-driven development is really a way of thinking. Some developers follow this approach and write tests first, while others write their own code first, and then tests. Then, there are those who do not write tests at all. If you fall into the latter category, then I hope that the methods you will learn in this chapter will help you start working in the right direction.

There are so many excuses not to write unit tests. For example, there was no question of a testing framework, or because of this, the development time will increase by 20%, or the tests are outdated, so we don't run them anymore. The truth is that these days we can't afford not to write tests. Applications grow in size and become more complex, and the requirements change over time. An application with a good set of tests can be changed much faster, and it will be much more resistant to future changes in requirements than an application that does not have tests. That is, when the real savings in unit testing costs become apparent. By writing unit tests for your application, you check its future and ensure that any change in the code base does not break the existing functionality. We also want to write our own applications, so that they stand the test of time. The code we are currently writing can be in a production environment for years, which means that sometimes you will have to make improvements or fix bugs in code that was written many years ago. If the application has a complete set of tests surrounding it, then changes can be made with confidence that these changes will not violate the existing functionality.

Test-driven development in the JavaScript space also adds another layer to our code coverage. Quite often, development teams write tests designed only for the application logic on the server side.

For example, in the Visual Studio space, these tests are often written only with a focus on the MVC framework, which consists of controllers, views, and basic business logic. It has always been quite difficult to test the application logic on the client side, in other words, the actual rendered HTML code and user interactions.

Frameworks for testing JavaScript code provide us with tools to address this gap. Now we can start modularizing our visualized HTML code, as well as modeling user interactions, such as filling out forms and clicking a button. This additional layer of testing, combined with server – side testing, means that we have a way to unit test every layer of our application-from server-side business logic to server-side page rendering, all the way down to user interaction. This ability to perform unit testing of user interactions with the client side of the interface is one of the most powerful aspects of any MV*JavaScript framework. In fact, it may even affect the architectural decisions you make when choosing a technology stack.

MODULE, INTEGRATION, AND ACCEPTANCE TESTINGS

Automated testing can be divided into three main areas, or types of testing: module testing, integration testing, and acceptance testing. You can also describe these testing as testing from the "black box" or from the "white box." White-box testings are those in which the internal logic or structure of the code under testing is known to the tester. Black-box testings, on the other hand, are those in which the internal design and/or logic is unknown to the tester.

Module Testings

A module testing is usually a white-box testing in which all the external interfaces of a code block are mocked or muted. If we are testing some code that, for example, performs an asynchronous call to load a JSON block, module testing of this code will require locking the returned JSON. This method ensures that the object under testing is always given a known set of data. When new requirements arise, this well-known data set can grow and expand, of course. The objects under testing should be designed to interact with interfaces, so that these interfaces can be easily mocked or silenced in a module testing scenario.

Integration Testings

Integration testings are another form of white-box testings that allow the object under testing to run in an environment close to real-world code. In our previous example, when some code executes an asynchronous call to load a JSON block, the integration testing actually needs to call the REST services that generate the JSON. If this REST service relies on data from the database, then the integration testing will require data in the database that matches the integration testing scenario. If we were to describe a module testing as having a boundary around the object under testing, then an integration testing is simply an extension of that boundary to include dependent objects or services.

Creating automated integration testings for your applications will significantly improve the quality of your product. Consider the case of the scenario we used when a block of code calls the REST service for data in JSON format. Someone can easily change the structure of this data returned by the REST service. Our unit testings will still pass, as they don't actually call the REST code on the server side, but our application will be messed up because the returned JSON doesn't meet our expectations.

Without integration testings, these types of errors will only be detected at later stages of manual testing. By thinking about integration testings, by implementing specific data sets for integration testings and embedding them in your own set, you can quickly eliminate such errors.

Acceptance Testings

Acceptance testings are black-box testings and are generally scenario-based. They can include multiple custom screens or custom interactions to pass through. These tests are also commonly performed by the test team, as they may require logging in to the application, searching for a specific dataset, updating data, and so on. Using planning and the many tools available, we can also automate these acceptance tests so that they run as part of an automated test suite. The more acceptance tests a project has, the more reliable it will be. Note that in the test-driven development methodology, each error detected by the manual testing team should lead to the creation of new unit, integration, or acceptance tests. This methodology will help ensure that once an error is found and fixed, it will not appear again.

REFACTORING

Refactoring is a systematic procedure for improving code without creating new functionality. Refactoring turns mess into clean code and simple design.

As trivial as it may sound, refactoring in a large project is a complicated thing, especially if the tests in the project are not written for every function or are written in such a way that they do not cover the entire code base or not all use cases. Even by slightly changing the behavior of a function, you always run the risk of returning something from it or passing (forgetting to pass) something wrong to it. This case is more in the piggy bank of tests, but still with TypeScript you can be sure that the function returns the type that you specified and accepts exactly what you specified.

TYPESCRIPT 4.2 RELEASE

Microsoft has released TypeScript 4.2. This is the most recent update at the time of writing this book. In the quarterly update of the language, it is now possible to set the abstract modifier to the constructor signature and mark the variable as unused when the array is destructured. Tuple types now allow rest arguments at any position, and type aliases are no longer expanded when a hint is displayed.

SUPPORT FOR REST ELEMENTS IN THE FIRST AND INTERMEDIATE PARAMETERS OF TUPLES OF TYPES

The tuple syntax in TypeScript supports rest elements that are prefixed with [...] and can contain any number of parameters of the same type. Previously, rest parameters were put in the last position, so it was impossible to express tuple types that end with a fixed set of elements. Such tuple types are useful for strongly typed functions with lists of variable parameters that end with a fixed set of parameters.

Tuple types now allow rest parameters at any position, not just the last one. For example:

```
type T1 = [...string [], number]; / / Zero or more
strings followed by a number;
type T2 = [number, ...boolean [], string, string]; / /
A number followed by zero or more boolean values
followed by two strings.
```

Now there is only one restriction for rest elements – they cannot go after other rest elements and before optional elements.

SAVING-TYPE ALIASES

Type aliases are now saved for more correct display of the hint in the IDE and type output in the .d.ts definition files. It also tracks type aliases for instances of other aliases. This makes the representation of composite types readable (including in the definition *file. d.ts*).

THE ABSTRACT MODIFIER IN CONSTRUCTOR SIGNATURES

TypeScript allows you to mark a class as abstract – in this case, it is only used to extend it with a subclass, and object instances are created only for a specific implementation class. But in TypeScript of previous versions, there were problems when creating mix-ins that use abstract classes.

TypeScript 4.2 allows you to specify an abstract modifier for constructor signatures. Adding an abstract modifier to the constructor signature signals that an abstract class can be passed to it. This does not prevent you from passing other classes and constructor functions that are "specific" to it.

Mix-in factories will now support abstract classes.

```
abstract class Shape {
    abstract getArea(): number;
}
// Error! You cannot create an instance of an abstract
class.
    new Shape();
interface HasArea {
    getArea(): number;
}
```

```
// Error! You cannot assign an abstract constructor
type to a non-abstract constructor type.
let Ctor: new () => HasArea = Shape;
// Works!
let Ctor: abstract new () => HasArea = Shape;
```

Strict Checks for the In Statement

In JavaScript, using a non-object type on the right side of the in statement is a runtime error. The syntax check in TypeScript 4.2 ensures that this error can be detected during development.

```
"foo" in 42
// Error! The right side of the in expression must
not be a primitive.
```

UNUSED VARIABLES DURING ARRAY DESTRUCTURIZATION

Now, when destructuring an array, you can explicitly mark variables as unused by adding an underscore to them.

```
let [_first, second] = getValues();
```

Previously, when the *noUnusedLocals* option was enabled, this syntax gave an error: "Variable declared, but not read." Now, for array variables that have an underscore prefix, the error will not be returned.

TYPE ARGUMENTS

Type arguments are not allowed in JavaScript, but in TypeScript 4.2, the parser will parse them in a specification-compliant way. When writing the following code in a JavaScript file:

```
f < T > (100)
```

TypeScript will parse it as:

```
(f < T) > (100)
```

This is important if you have used the TypeScript API to analyze type constructs in JavaScript files.

In addition, there is a new *noPropertyAccessFromIndexSignature* option. This function disables the ability to use a point to access those object properties that are defined using the string index signature.

If there is a function inside the Boolean expressions with && and ||
without calling it, this will result in a compilation error under the – *strict-
NullChecks flag.*

In the newest version of TypeScript, they also added support for the -
explainFiles flag. You can use it to understand why the file was included in
the compilation process.

Future Plans

The next quarterly version of TypeScript 4.3 was released on May 25.
The iteration plan lists upcoming language features, editor performance
improvements, performance improvements, infrastructure improvements, and more.

In addition, according to the TypeScript roadmap, Microsoft plans to:

• Allow any key type as an index signature parameter

• Add keywords –noImplicitOverride and override

• Add a static index signature

• Use unknown as the type for the catch clause variables

• Allow more code before super () calls in subclasses

• Allow typeof to follow the class expression

Remember that in 2020, Microsoft revealed the source code of the
TypeScript library for editing documents in the cloud.

CHAPTER 6

Appraisal

Typescript is both a language and a set of tools for generating JavaScript code. It was developed by Anders Heilsberg at Microsoft Corporation to help developers write enterprise-wide JavaScript code. This book begins with an introduction to the Typescript language, and gradually moves from basic concepts to advanced and powerful features of the language, including asynchronous programming methods, decorators, and generalizations. Many modern JavaScript and Typescript frameworks are also considered in parallel. Some of the well-known object-oriented methods and design patterns are described, and their real-world implementations are presented. Using this book, you can create a comprehensive, end-to-end web application that shows you how to combine Typescript features, design patterns, and best development practices in a real-world scenario.

Typescript is a very powerful tool that allows you to significantly improve the readability and security of your code. In this book, we have looked at Typescript both inside and out. In the first chapter of this book, we compared JavaScript with Typescript and noted the strengths of Typescript. Typescript is statistically typed and this makes it easier to use. In addition to this, statistical typing has such a feature as auto-completion in code editors, which makes the process of writing code easier, because you do not need to constantly look through the documentation and search for the name of the method you need. After that, we moved on to the part where we analyzed how ECMAScript works with Typescript. Typescript is a compiled superset of JavaScript, bringing optional static typing and some of the features of modern ECMAScript standards. The Typescript compiler has a parameter that can switch between different versions of the ECMAScript standard and currently TypeScript supports ES3, ES5, and ES6.

Also, in parallel, a lot of modern JavaScript and TypeScript frameworks are considered – for each of them, module and integration testing is described in detail. Some of the well-known object-oriented methods and design patterns are described, and their real-world implementations are presented.

TypeScript brings many benefits to developer productivity and developer experience. TypeScript is not unique to Angular, other powerful frontend frameworks such as React are beginning to be used with TypeScript to allow development teams to build robust, resilient, and scalable applications. JavaScript and TypeScript are constantly evolving but do not compete with each other. TypeScript was created to complement and improve JavaScript, not to replace it. In the future, they may become very similar in their functions, but TypeScript will remain a statically typed alternative.

If you're new to JavaScript, you shouldn't grin at the first mention of TypeScript. TypeScript was developed not just to encourage backend developers to work with the frontend, but to build on lessons learned from other languages to provide everyone with a tool that allows you to create reliable code.

JavaScript was created to be portable and simple – but over time, we have seen that the language goes beyond its original intent. Although a few hundred, if not thousands of lines of code, could still be supported in regular JavaScript – we all know that this is no longer the case. JavaScript code works everywhere and on almost every device. The number of rows is growing exponentially, and we need a way to mentally digest and maintain it.

It is not difficult to learn TypeScript itself. It is written and runs like JavaScript – with only a few tools and techniques to help you improve the code. In fact, you can just write TypeScript code like JavaScript, and it will still compile. While TypeScript may seem like syntactic sugar, it makes our experience of maintaining and writing code much more optimal.

I hope that by the end of this book, you will be able to create a comprehensive, end-to-end web application that shows you how to combine TypeScript features, design patterns, and best practices in a real-world scenario.

Appendix

Types

String	let customerName: string= "John Doe";
Number	let price: number = 19.95;
Boolean	let shipped: boolean = false;
Date	let orderDate: Date = new Date(2017, 2, 9);
Any	let something: any = "Can be anything";
Enum	enum Color {Red, Green, Blue};
Array	let cards: string[] = ['Visa', 'MasterCard'];
Null	let orderId: number = null;
Tuple	let stateTaxRates: [string, number];
Void	function log(msg: string): void { console.log(msg); }
Const	const lives: number = 99;

Usage

Installing TypeScript npm	npm install -g typescript
Compiling TypeScript	tsc somefile.ts
TypeScript Docs	TypeScriptLang.org
Type Definition Files	DefinatelyTyped.org

Scope/Modifiers

Public (default)	public firstName: string;
Protected	protected inventory: number;
Private	private outOfStock: boolean;
Read Only	readonly pi: number = 3.14159;
Static	static log(msg: string) { console.log(msg) };

Classes

```
class OrderLogic {
  constructor(public order: IOrder) { }

  getOrderTotal(): number {
      let sum: number = 0;

      for (let orderDetail of this.order.
orderDetails)
      {
          sum += orderDetail.price;
      }
      return sum;
  }
}
```

Abstract Classes

```
abstract class Person {
  name: string;
  monthlySalary: number;
  monthlyBenefits: number;

  abstract calcSalary(): number;
}
```

Interfaces

```
interface IOrderDetail {
  productName: string;
  quantity: number;
  price: number;
  orderDate: Date;
  shipped: boolean;
  //Optional
  outOfStock?: boolean;
  //Method
  calcTax: (taxRate: number) => number;
}
```

Inheritance and Implementing Interfaces

```
interface IGPS {
  getLocation() number;
}
```

```typescript
interface ISelfDrive extends IGPS {
  drive(latitude: number, longitude: number,
elevation: number): void;
}

class Vehicle {
  make: string;
  model: string;
  year: number;
}

class FlyingCar extends Vehicle implements ISelfDrive
{
  hasGps: boolean;

  drive(latitude: number, longitude: number,
elevation: number) {
  }

  getLocation(): number {
  }
}
```

Optional Parameters

```typescript
class Util {
  log(msg: string, logDate?: Date) {
    if (logDate)
      console.log(logDate + ' ' + msg);
    else
      console.log(new Date() + ' ' + msg);
  }
}
```

Rest Parameters

```typescript
class Order {
  addOrderDetails(...orderDetails: IOrderDetail[]) {
  }
}
```

Namespaces

```typescript
namespace AcmeCorp.Logging {
  export class Logger {
```

```
        static log(msg: string): void {
        console.log(msg);
        };
  }
}

/// <reference path="AcmeCorp.Logging.ts" />

//Alias
import logger = AcmeCorp.Logging.Logger;

namespace AcmeCorp.OnlineStore {
  class OrderLogic {
    calcOrder(): number {
        logger.log("calculating order");
        return 0;
    }
  }
}
```

Triple Slash Directives

Reference built-in types	/// <reference lib="es2016.array.include" /> /// <reference path="../my_types" />
Reference other types	/// <reference types="jquery" />
AMD	/// <amd-module name="Name" /> /// <amd-dependency path="app/foo" name="foo" />

Compiler Comments

Don't check this file	// @ts-nochec
Check this file	// @ts-check
Igonre the next line	// @ts-ignore
Expect an error on the next line	// @ts-expect-error

Index

Printed in the United States
by Baker & Taylor Publisher Services